From Fruit Trees to Furnaces

A History of the Worcestershire Constabulary

By

Bob Pooler

Published by:

**Blacksmith Publishing
The Paddock
Lower Moor
Pershore
Worcs
WR10 2PA
United Kingdom**

Any infringement of copyright is unintentional,
and every effort has been made to ensure
that this has not occurred.

© Copyright R.J. Pooler 2002

All rights reserved.
No part of this publication may be reproduced,
stored in a retrieval system,
or transmitted, in any form, or by any means,
electronic, mechanical, photocopying, recording or otherwise,
without the prior written permission of the publisher.

From Fruit Trees to Furnaces
A History of the Worcestershire Constabulary

Contents

Chapter One   Page 7
A new beginning, The first chief constable, The superintendents and constables, Getting to work, Early press liaison, Sergeants are appointed, Some public discontent, A new building programme, Police, criminals and crime, More opposition, Problems for the chief constable, Changes at Evesham.

Chapter Two   Page 19
Violent times, Unsatisfactory wages, Poor accommodation, Superannuation scheme, Working conditions, Conference points, Rewards for good work, An error of judgement, First government inspection, The first detective.

Chapter Three   Page 28
The railway, An increase in responsibilities, A question of judgement, a new uniform design, Public appreciation, Mundane duties, Retirement of the first chief constable and his deputy.

Chapter Four   Page 34
A new leader, Problem policemen, Recruiting and training, Society for the prevention of cruelty to animals, The Blockley riot, Droitwich and Bewdley forces absorbed, The murder of a policeman.

Chapter Five   Page 45
A new police authority, An embarrassing affair, A former policeman – bad through and through, Unacceptable behaviour, Nurse Elizabeth, Murder of a gamekeeper.

Chapter Six   Page 58
A statutory pension, New boundaries – new buildings, A nasty murder, Merit badges and rewards, Injuries to policemen, A wage review, Boer War, Departure of the deputy chief constable, Communications, The first intake.

Chapter Seven   Page 73
Death of Lt. Col. Carmichael, A new broom, Motor cars, Road accidents, Young offenders and poor children, Public counters, A commission of enquiry, There was good work too, A mounted branch, Election time at Droitwich, Birmingham expands – again, A close call.

Chapter Eight   Page 83
Changes in transport, First World War, The return of peace – Demobilisation, Police Constable Frederick Hayes, A police union - but not for long, The last execution at Worcester gaol.

Chapter Nine   Page 94
Dudley, Superintendent Charles Rudnick.

Chapter Ten   Page 104
Memorial to the fallen, Industrial unrest, Married life for a policeman, Women and the Worcestershire Constabulary, Policewomen, Telephones, Typists and typewriters, Prisoner transport, On patrol in the 1920s and 30s

Chapter Eleven   Page 114
New law, fresh demands, Motor patrol, Superintendent Peter Mobbs, PC Stanley Hill, More boundary changes, Walker's departure, Captain J. E. Lloyd-Williams, Wage reductions, Police family traditions, The wind of change, More heroic work, Dr Oliver Terry F.R.C.P., The Second World War, Disabled police officers, A courageous bobby, The murder of Florrie Porter, The Bella mystery, Counting the cost of war.

Chapter Twelve   Page 137
Kidderminster, Bad weather , good work, A dangerous domestic, Hindlip Hall, A keen sense of humour, Police cadets, Police dogs, Cyprus, Police officers out and about, Lloyd-Williams retires, Worcestershire's last chief constable, New-style uniforms, County motorways, Police bravery, A new police station at Malvern, Reduction in the working week, A Police Authority, A new police force, The Hindlip fire, The end of the Worcestershire Constabulary.

FOREWORD

**By the last Chief Constable of the Worcestershire Constabulary
(1958-1967)
and Chief Constable of the West Mercia Constabulary
(1967-1974)
Sir John Willison OBE, QPM, DL**

It requires great determination to write any book, but to assemble the facts from a period of almost 130 years and to incorporate them into a readable book is a monumental achievement. Bob Pooler has done so and Worcestershire Constabulary will now be properly documented for the first time.

The Police Service draws a great deal of its strength from its traditions and of the splendid men who have devoted their lives to the service. At the same time those in the service must be aware of the changing conditions in society and attune the service to those changes.

This book shows how Worcestershire has met these challenges over the years.

John Willison

From Fruit Trees to Furnaces

A History of the Worcestershire Constabulary

Introduction

This book is the result of more than twelve years research into the history of the Worcestershire Constabulary. In the first draft I tried to incorporate nearly all of the information that I had gathered. This proved to be an unreadable collection of facts and names covering nearly five hundred pages. It was therefore, with some regret, that I had to prune the detail into a form which I hope is more acceptable. Inevitably this has meant leaving out a number of events, and the names of many officers who have contributed to the Worcestershire Police story.

The gathering of material has led to numerous enjoyable meetings with many interesting and pleasant people. Some were former police officers or civilian employees, whilst others were relatives of policemen from many years ago. They were all, without exception, generous with their time and recollections. There are far too many to mention, but I am grateful to you all, thank you.

Over the years I have been able to build up a large collection of photographs in which either police officers are the main subject or form part of the scene photographed. I am indebted to the many people who have sent me photographs, or allowed me to copy those they wished to retain. A selection of photographs from the collection appear in this book and as far as I am aware there should not be any copyright problems, however any errors in this respect will be mine.

I found the County Record Office at Worcester, a number of the county libraries and the West Mercia Police Heritage Centre to be excellent sources of information. I would especially like to thank Tony Wherry and Robin Whittaker from the Worcestershire County Record Office for making special arrangements for me to view certain records. I am also extremely grateful to successive Chief Constables of the West Mercia Constabulary and especially to curator Lydia Warner and her successor Helen Marsh, both of whom were generous with their time and in making records available.

I am indebted to Ann Brennan who was kind enough to read the manuscript and make many constructive comments. Last, but not least, I must thank my son Matt, whose help throughout this project has clarified many clouded issues and identified numerous officers contained in anonymous photographs some of which are shown in this book.

This is the first time that a history of the police in Worcestershire has been published and I hope that it provides interest to both police history enthusiasts and others who enjoy a good read.

Bob Pooler
Pershore

Part I

Chapter One

From Fruit Trees to Furnaces

A History of the Worcestershire Constabulary

A new beginning

The sight of a police uniform on the highways and byways of Worcestershire has long been taken for granted. Many would say it is not common enough, a few that it was rather unfortunate. For most of us, though, the uniform offers an everyday reassurance, and on occasions an absolute lifeline.

At the beginning of the nineteenth century the existing policing system had been in place for over five hundred years. Few people could have guessed at the changes that would soon occur and at the effect a uniformed police force would have on their lives. Some citizens may have heard of the Bow Street Runners, the Horse Patrols and the Thames Marine Police, but these were in London, a world away from the inhabitants of Worcestershire for whom the title 'constable' still meant the parish official whose ancient office went back to medieval times. The constable, originally an officer of the township or tithing – a 'headborough' or 'tithingman' – became the principal executive officer in the parish, and was required to bring before the justice of the peace those people who had offended in any way.

A lot was expected of the parish constable. As well as exercising his common law powers of arrest, he was required to attend to paupers and vagrants, and even to report on the morals of his neighbours. He also had duties relating to parish apprentices, wages and working hours; and in some areas a further responsibility of keeping an eye on the state of the roads and bridges. Only knights, clergymen and women were exempt from this onerous office, which, much to the annoyance of business people appointed to the post, went largely unpaid.

Not surprisingly, the elected constable often preferred to assign his duties to a deputy, and sometimes the latter would also look for a stand-in, a practice that greatly reduced efficiency. At times, and within its limitations, the local policing system had worked reasonably well, but by the nineteenth century the country was undergoing huge changes. Under pressure from a growing population, which was more affluent and mobile, the old system was creaking towards breaking point.

The introduction of the police force we see today is credited to Sir Robert Peel. On 29th September 1829, a uniformed force totalling one thousand men marched onto the streets of London. Once the Metropolitan Police was established there was no going back. Prominent citizens in the provinces were determined to introduce police forces into their own areas as well. In Worcestershire, a prime mover was local MP Sir John Pakington. Born John Somerset Russell on 20th February 1799, he was the son of William Russell of Powick Court near Worcester. Upon the death of his maternal uncle, Sir John Pakington, he inherited the Pakington family estates, and on the 14th March 1831 he changed his name from Russell to Pakington. After a number of failed attempts he was eventually returned as the parliamentary representative for Droitwich in July 1837, and served as chairman of the Court of Quarter Sessions until 1858. Pakington held his parliamentary seat until 1874 when, following defeat in the general election, he was created Baron Hampton of Hampton Lovett and Westwood. He died in London on 9th April 1880 at the age of eighty-one and is buried at the family mausoleum at Hampton Lovett church.

Even before the Metropolitan Police came into existence, a number of towns in Worcestershire had organised patrols to keep the peace and to prevent crime. One of the earliest recorded was at Kidderminster in 1823 where a 'Night Watch' operated from 9.45p.m.until 5.00a.m. The watchmen were equipped with a lanthorn (a form of lantern), staff and rattle and they were required to call the hour and half-hour throughout the night. At least the criminals knew where they were.

In February 1824 the City of Worcester took on eight watchmen at a salary of 12/6 (62½p) per week in the summer and an extra 1/- (5p) in the winter 'for candle'. Redditch called their law enforcers 'Night Patrol', and in 1827, Charles Swann, W. Bartleet, Joseph Turner senior and junior were instructed to attend from 'twelve till five' or forfeit one pound. In the same year Dudley took on four watchmen at a salary of 12/- (60p) per week. They were William Baird, Joseph Southall, James Farren, and Thomas Neale. James Robinson was appointed as their superintendent at 5/- (25p) per week. Each watchman was supplied with appropriate clothing, a lanthorn and a rattle. It wasn't long before the watchmen were in need of watching because of their negligence and drunkenness.

In 1831 Redditch suffered the attentions of a gang of criminals who were able to operate daily with impunity. To combat the problem, special constables were sworn in, and at night the town's streets were lit by oil lamps. This led to a sharp reduction in crime. Economic pressures resulted in the oil lamps being turned off, and, as a consequence the number of crimes began to rise again. The special constables became the butts of many jokes. One example was, "our constables don't need to be vaccinated, they never catch anything."

In these times of extreme lawlessness it was far beyond the capabilities of the parish constables to control most criminal events. Violence and crime were commonplace.

Rioting occurred in many major cities, including Worcester, and the authorities were forced to rely upon the military to keep the peace.

There were changes in law enforcement in 1835 when the Municipal Corporations Act gave boroughs the opportunity to set up their own police forces. Kidderminster started in that year, followed by Worcester, Bewdley, Droitwich and Evesham in 1836. These forces came under the control of watch committees to whom the chief or head constable reported. However, policing in the remainder of the county remained a very haphazard affair.

On 8th April 1839, the Court of Quarter Sessions - the authority responsible for maintaining law and order in the county, and chaired by Pakington concluded that a police force was essential for the county. Events taking place in adjacent districts and further afield provided a convincing argument, if such was necessary, to persuade any doubters of the need for a police force. Supporters of Chartism, a movement for political reform, were causing serious disturbances across the country and their activities were regularly reported in local papers. At the same time, local crime appeared to be spiralling out of control.

A police committee was formed under the chairmanship of Sir John Pakington, and it met for the first time on Saturday 2nd November 1839. The members were men of considerable influence and means, and were drawn from the county magistracy. They included Thomas Badger from Dudley, Richard Spooner, Reverend Anthony Berwick Lechmere of Upton, Lieutenant General Thomas Marriott of Pershore, John Williams of Pitmaston, Reverend Thomas Pearson from Hundred House, William Trow from Kidderminster, Henry Talbot, William Henry Ricketts and William Evans.

The first chief constable

The first task of the police committee was to appoint a chief constable. Advertisements for the post appeared in three London newspapers, the *United Services Gazette* and all Worcester newspapers. There were thirty-two applications for the position, including twenty retired army officers, five police officers, a gaoler, a bailiff, a workhouse manager and an eating house manager. One applicant, Christopher Kempster from London, missed the closing date for applications and took the unusual course of alerting the Justices to his existence by making an application in the form of a letter, which was published by the *Worcester Herald* on 30th November 1839. There is no evidence that his application was entertained.

To qualify for selection, the applicant had to be of sound health and character with the ability to read, write and keep books. A man under forty-five years of age, with these qualities, and appointed to the post could expect to receive a salary of two hundred and fifty pounds per annum plus expenses.

The committee reduced the field to a shortlist of five, before finally and unanimously choosing a Metropolitan Police inspector named Richard Reader Harris as the first Chief Constable of Worcestershire.

Harris was a married man and had at least one child, a son also named Richard Reader Harris. Little is known of Harris' early life, but Metropolitan Police archives show that he had completed five years' service when he was appointed inspector at the age of thirty. In October 1839, six months after his promotion to inspector, he was assisting in recruiting men for the newly formed Birmingham Borough Police. However, it was Harris' experience in the investigative field that ensured his appointment. He came with glowing testimonials concerning his work on a serious case of arson in Lincolnshire and a murder near Truro in Cornwall.

Harris took his oath of office on 16th December 1839, placing the Worcestershire Constabulary amongst the first of the county police forces to be created. The business of setting up and running a police force was an extremely complicated affair. There was limited expertise available for a novice chief constable to draw upon, whilst his employers had high expectations from the moment he was appointed. As well as recruiting suitable men for the force, it was necessary to find them accommodation, order their uniforms and ensure that they were properly equipped. The men then had to be trained and effectively deployed across the county.

Richard Reader Harris
The first Chief Constable of the Worcestershire Constabulary
1839 - 1871

The superintendents and constables

Ten superintendents were the first to be recruited, all of whom had some background in law enforcement. The constables were taken on in two batches, totalling thirty men. The first group arrived on Boxing Day 1839, with the remainder ten days later. These recruits had to be under forty years of age, at least 5' 7" (170cms) without shoes, literate, intelligent and active. The character of these men had to be irreproachable and supported by references - all for 19/- (95p) a week. The difficulty in establishing the backgrounds of some recruits meant that mistakes were made. A number were poachers turned gamekeepers. Their lack of personal discipline, coupled with being part of a national propensity to abuse alcohol, was to lead, in part, to a rapid turnover of policemen for much of the remainder of the century.

A Worcester doctor, Matthew Pierpoint, was appointed as the police surgeon. He was initially employed to medically examine the new recruits before they were accepted into the force. He was paid 2/6d (12½p) for each examination; this was later increased to 5/- (25p).

The recruits faced a three-week course at the Shirehall in Worcester before they were allowed to face the public. This basic training included the teaching of drill and criminal law, and provided details of police powers and the operating procedures of the force. A number of the trainees received assistance with their general education, which included copying standard phrases used in police reports. The training broadly followed the blueprint given in a Home Office instruction manual, a copy of which was given to each officer.

It was during this training period that the men were issued with their uniforms and equipment. The uniform was similar to that worn by Metropolitan Police officers and included a stove pipe hat with a leather top and a blue tailcoat with darker blue or black trousers. Each officer was allocated an individual number that was clearly displayed on the upright collar of the tailcoat, alongside the county arms. A broad leather belt was buckled over the tailcoat and a caped greatcoat was worn in inclement weather. The outfit was rounded off with a pair of leather boots or shoes.

Their equipment included a wooden truncheon, a rattle (which was later replaced by a whistle) and a lantern that could be carried on the belt. Handcuffs were issued late in 1840. Officers on night duty were permitted to carry a small cutlass; this weapon was also issued to them if there was a fear of public disorder.

When their training period was completed on Friday 24th January 1840, the new police officers were assembled to hear an address by the chief constable and a 'pep' talk by John Williams, a police committee member. They were then sent away to their beats to prepare for duty on the following Monday.

The police stations, mainly rented cottages, were not always located at the centres of population that one would expect. Whilst most reasonably sized towns not operating their own police force, such as Stourbridge and Bromsgrove, were catered for, country districts including Rock, Upton Snodsbury, Leigh and Birtsmorton were also allocated a policeman. In fact, the police cottages were chosen more for their positions, on or near main roads, rather than any other reason.

The county police headquarters were established at 15 Britannia Square, Worcester and were initially known as the 'Central Depot for the Police'. The chief clerk, Superintendent Peter Allez, lived there, whilst Harris lived on the other side of Britannia Square, but he soon made his home at The Grange, St. Johns, Worcester. Later still, he lived at 'Rowallan', Avenue Road, Great Malvern, conveniently close to the railway station. The central depot had no cell accommodation, so prisoners had to be secured at the Worcester City police station.

The salaries of the chief constable and his superintendents were sufficient to provide them with an extremely comfortable lifestyle, which included employing domestic staff. The force allowed each of them to have an orderly, and he was a policeman who acted as a groom and batman.

Getting to work

Without doubt, the new constables were thrown in at the deep end. They were carrying out unfamiliar duties in a largely hostile environment, but, they were a tenacious bunch. On Monday 10th February 1840, which, coincidentally, happened to be Queen Victoria's wedding day, PC Edward Davis from Upton Snodsbury, in the Pershore division, received a complaint concerning the theft of 29lbs (13kgs) of bacon from innkeeper John Crocker of Crowle. PC Davis soon arrested Henry Lampit, who was a navvy working on the construction of the Birmingham to Gloucester railway line. A gang of Lampit's workmates armed themselves with sticks and attacked the policeman, forcing him to let Lampit go. Undeterred, Davis gathered together colleagues from both the city and the county police, and was able to recapture his prisoner at the Hole in the Wall beerhouse in Droitwich. Lampit received six months' imprisonment.

On another occasion, early the following year, Superintendent William Manton of Pershore pursued poacher Thomas Hooper to Croydon, where he arrested him. Hooper was wanted for shooting and wounding one of the Earl of Coventry's gamekeepers.

In August 1842, PC John Raby was assaulted by waterboatman George Clay at Upton. Raby had heard of a disturbance brewing, so he took off his uniform jacket and mingled with the mob. He was injured as he tried to stop a fight involving Clay. At a later court hearing, Clay was fined 2/6d (12½p) with 6/- (30p) costs, whilst Raby was reprimanded by the chairman of the bench for discarding his uniform, instead of preventing the disturbance by wearing it.

Borough policemen were also confronted with difficult situations. In one incident, Inspector Arton of the Evesham Borough police had an uncomfortable experience when he found himself at the wrong end of a loaded gun whilst trying to arrest fowl stealers William and John Grinnell of Three Cocks Lane, Offenham. Arton eventually managed to take possession of the gun and arrest the thieves, without injury to himself. Both offenders were later sentenced to twelve months' in solitary confinement in the county gaol.

Offenders could expect little sympathy from the courts, and harsh sentences were regularly handed down by the magistracy. Dishonest policemen were similarly dealt with. In 1841, PC John Hughes pleaded guilty to drinking in a beerhouse at Harvington for eight hours, and to making false entries about his duties. He was fined £5.00d with 6/6d (32½p) costs and allowed three days to pay, or had to face an alternative of one month in gaol with hard labour. It is difficult to see how he could pay a fine of almost six weeks' wages without getting into debt, but this observation is academic as he was dismissed from the force shortly afterwards.

Chief Superintendent Henry Burton
Photo: c1885

Early press liaison

Superintendent John Lane, later to become deputy chief constable, was one of the first Worcestershire policemen to encounter the press. It happened early in 1840, when Upton upon Severn was cut off because of flooding. Lane was the police officer in charge of the area. One day he was joined in a rowing boat by a reporter, from the *Worcestershire Chronicle,* who wished to view the floods. For some reason an disagreement arose between them, and it only concluded when the reporter fell out of the boat into the river.

The exact circumstances of the incident are not known, but when the chief constable got to hear about it, he moved Lane to Worcester and replaced him with a trusted friend, Superintendent Henry Burton. Probably, a safer pair of hands in early public relations were required at the Old Street police station.

Sergeants are appointed

Dismissals and resignations of constables were soon running at such a level that the thin blue line was in severe danger of becoming dotted. The force was finding out just how difficult it was to recruit and retain men of the right calibre and staying power. When eight sergeants were appointed in November 1840 they had to be used to supplement rather than supervise the constables.

Matters got so bad that even former policemen with an unsatisfactory service history were taken on as sergeants. Joseph Radford was a constable in the first draft of policemen in December 1839. By late 1841 he had been appointed sergeant. In November of that year he went drinking with two constables, at a hostelry at Corse Lawn. Some time later the three of them were found brawling at Eldersfield. The incident resulted in one of the constables being assaulted. Each of the policemen appeared before Harris to be disciplined. Radford was fined £1, moved to another station and reduced to the rank of constable. He resigned from the force a couple of months later. Within four months Joseph Radford re-applied to join the force. He was accepted and immediately appointed to the rank of sergeant. He served until his retirement in 1857.

During this time the superintendents must have felt that they were never off duty. They worked as criminal investigators, administrators and managers, and still had to be available to receive prisoners at any time, day or night.

Some public discontent

Compared to today's standards the cost of running the force was minuscule. However the sum involved, four to five thousand pounds per annum, was totally borne by county ratepayers, some of whom found their contributions both painful and unnecessary. Voices of protest began to be heard across the county. There were declarations that the police force was inefficient and too costly. Some wealthy rural landowners spoke angrily of having to pay for policing urban areas where the risk of crime and disorder was far greater than in the countryside. Behind the scenes, Sir John Pakington struggled to make the bitter pill of the county police rate more palatable. He pressed the government to share the expense of operating the police force by contributing one third of the disbursements. In the meantime, the police rate was set at ¼d (0.10416p) in the pound on all rateable properties in the county. By comparison, at the same time a ½d (0.20833p) rate was set to raise funds to build the county hall and courts of justice, with lodgings for HM Justices of Assize.

The ratepayers of Halesowen refused to pay the police rate for some time. Although Halesowen was a detached part of Salop, the Worcestershire Constabulary policed the area with a superintendent and a constable. When the arrears had reached £74.16.11d (£74.84½) the Court of Quarter Sessions lost all patience and threatened enforcement proceedings. The Halesowen authorities decided to pay up.

At Chaddesley Corbett, a group of ratepayers banded together to try and get the constabulary disbanded, or at the very least suspended, until the ratepayers were able to support it. The parish subsequently set up an association for the detection of felons, which relied heavily upon both the efficiency of the parish constables and a system of financial rewards. These associations were not new and had operated for a number of years in other parts of the county with moderate success, but only for its members. However, whilst the police force was in place these alliances were destined to fail.

Opponents of the police force were presented with an unexpected opportunity in December 1841 when the *Berrows Worcester Journal* reported a rumour that Harris intended to resign and take up an important post elsewhere. The ensuing call to get rid of the county police at the same time came to rather an abrupt halt when Harris announced he had no intention of leaving.

A new building programme

In 1841 the police committee embarked on a building programme designed to provide a number of county-owned station houses. Finding suitable premises had been a problem from the beginning. In Bromsgrove, for example, a thatched workhouse in the Strand was converted into a lock-up with four cells. Former parish constable Superintendent James King and a constable were stationed there. Bromsgrove, together with Kings Heath and Worcester, were each earmarked for new stations. A budget of between £400 and £500 was set for each project, which included office space, stabling and accommodation for both the superintendent and a constable, along with their families. A plot of land was identified in Station Street for the Bromsgrove station house, whilst at Worcester, Loves Grove alongside the county gaol was chosen. At Kings Heath, the tenancy for the existing premises was due to expire in July 1842. Although a site had not been identified, there were compelling reasons for new premises, not least the fact that two prisoners had tunnelled out of the unsuitable cell block and made good their escape.

By 1843 the search for accommodation was well on course. In March, the Stourport police occupied rented property at the canal basin, whilst at Malvern plans were prepared for a new station house to be built. Meanwhile, money was set aside for improvements at Stourbridge police station and for three cells to be added to the new police headquarters in Worcester.

Police, criminals and crime

Bentley wrote in his county almanac of 1842 that the county police have "...now attained a state of considerable efficiency - and the protection of life and property in this county, night and day appears to require the labours of 112 men and the annual cost of them to the public is £8,030...". The figures that Bentley used included the staffing costs of the borough police forces as well as those of the county. Droitwich had two officers, Dudley had eleven, Evesham three (some sources suggest there were six), Kidderminster had ten and Worcester twenty. The combined expenditure of the smaller forces was put at £2,530. By this time the authorised strength of the county force had risen to sixty-five. Bentley made no reference to Bewdley although there were two part-time policemen employed there. These men, who probably did not wear a uniform, were poorly paid and allowed to work at their own trades in order to supplement their police wages.

If Bentley based his views of police efficiency upon the numbers of defendants passing before the Courts of Assize and Quarter Sessions, then his assertions are well supported. Figures for 1821 show a total of 247 persons appearing before these courts. Twenty years later the figure had almost doubled. During the same period, convictions for minor offences grew from 292 to 461.

Bentley then examined how crime affected the county and how it fitted in with the national pattern. To achieve this, he obtained the details of inmates in the county gaol. He established that about one-third of the prisoners did not normally live in the county. Of the remainder, he found that Bewdley had the highest proportion of criminals per head of population, with Rock Forest particularly identified as a criminal district. There were nine Tenbury criminals in the prison, which was a greater proportion than any other part of the county. It transpired that five of them were from the same family. Upton upon Severn offences seemed to be committed by young offenders, whilst Malvern and Pershore criminals tended to be older. The violent atmosphere in Dudley meant that 'crimes against the person' in that town exceeded crimes against property. There were also more women offenders from that district than elsewhere. Stourbridge had a less than average number of crimes but a higher proportion of women in prison. Returns for Bewdley indicated that criminals were of the proportion 1 in 174 of the population, whilst at Shipston on Stour the figure was 1 in 639.

The Bentley study showed that there were three-times as many public houses as there were schools in the county, with six-times the expenditure going into the pubs compared with into education. The number of schools in Worcestershire was proportionate to the rest of England, and, in Bentley's opinion, a lack of education was an important factor in the criminal group he studied.

The arrest of criminals in other parts of England had risen by 8.3% over a five-year period, whilst in Worcestershire there was an increase of twice as much. The police committee proudly reported at the 1842 Epiphany Quarter Sessions that such figures reflected the efficiency of the police force. However, it was expenditure rather than statistics that determined the decision of the Quarter Sessions to refuse an increase in manpower.

More opposition

Whilst the members of the police committee looked to expand the force, others had very different thoughts. In 1842, a deputation of six magistrates, led by Dr Beale Cooper of Bengeworth, Evesham, presented a proposal to the Michaelmas Quarter Sessions, which if implemented would result in the county police force being pruned so severely that it would become totally impotent. Pakington and the committee were caught completely off guard and the meeting proved to be an extremely tough one. The political prowess of the chairman showed itself when he managed to get the proposition referred to the police committee, to consider and report upon, at the next sessions. He also displayed a stroke of genius when he proposed that the rebel magistrates, including Cooper, be co-opted onto the police committee. By the time the committee reported back to the Court of Quarter Sessions, the venom of the opponents had disappeared and their ambitions were never realised.

Problems for the chief constable

In January 1843, the police committee decided to trim its budget by reducing pay for some constables from 19/- (95p) to 16/- (80p) a week. The chief constable was allowed the discretion of applying the ruling to the officers he selected, but the overall effect was that about twenty-two men would be poorer. A transparent gesture to allow officers with a record of good conduct to earn higher wages did little to ease the bitterness created within the ranks.

Drawing conclusions, well after events have occurred, can be a risky business. A study of the chief constable appears to reveal him as a compassionate but occasionally indecisive man, lacking attention to administrative detail. It is highly likely that some of his superintendents had strong personalities and were often testing the boundaries within which Harris allowed them to operate. On one occasion, Harris approached the committee to seek its support concerning the transfer of a superintendent. He was quite properly told that the decision was his. In another instance, he received some strong advice from the police committee, when it was revealed that constables escorting prisoners to the county gaol kept their (the prisoner's) possessions, in the hope, naively perhaps, that they were all returned upon release. Property was, and still is, a thorny problem for police officers, and this scenario was no exception with its potential for dishonesty. Although the practice was widely known, Harris did nothing to prevent it occurring until he was instructed to do so. On yet another occasion in 1843, Harris was unable to satisfactorily answer a question put to him by the chairman of the police committee. He had been asked why a constable was found to be covering twelve parishes. The chairman sharply rebuked him for "displaying such ignorance of the statistics of your duty".

One of Harris' 'problem' superintendents was William Craig, and it was probably he who was the subject of the chief constable's application to the police committee mentioned previously. Craig was formerly the chief parish constable for Stourbridge. He lived in the house adjoining the town lock-up and had made a comfortable living by receiving rewards and fees in relation to his duties, serving warrants and escorting prisoners to Worcester. He had unsuccessfully applied for the post of chief constable of the county, and eventually accepted the role of police superintendent at Stourbridge. Craig was well connected at Stourbridge, probably too well connected to be the local chief of police. An attempt to move him to Upton upon Severn ran into all sorts of difficulties, not least his refusal to move out of his house at Stourbridge, the ownership of which had by now passed into the hands of the police authority. Then Craig resigned from the force in May 1842, and it became necessary to evict him to enable the new superintendent, Henry Burton, to move into the premises.

Changes at Evesham

A couple of years later, the head of the Evesham Borough police, Inspector William Arton, clashed with his police authority, but his difficulties were of a more terminal nature.

In January 1844 he was suspended for two weeks when he fought with his wife in front of the guests at the Oddfellows Ball, which was being held at the town hall. He compounded this transgression by failing to act on the Mayor's instructions and close the hall at 4.00a.m. Instead, he switched off the gas lighting at 6.30a.m. causing great confusion as the Ball was still in full swing. At a subsequent watch committee meeting, with implied understatement, Inspector Arton's language at the Ball was described as discourteous. The situation did not improve because at the beginning of August he submitted his resignation, but before it could take effect he was dismissed for neglect of duty and disorderly conduct.

Arton had started his law enforcement life as a watchman at Worcester. He served in the role for three years before joining the newly formed City police as a sergeant. Throughout his time at Worcester he was known as William Aston, but when he moved to Evesham as the Inspector on 1st February 1836, either by design or spelling error he became William Arton.

In July, 1849, an opportunity arose for Harris to expand the county force by absorbing the Worcester City police, following the death of its chief constable, Inspector John Phillips. Unfortunately his overtures were firmly rejected by the City watch committee. He had better luck with the Evesham authorities and reached an agreement in which a county police sergeant and one constable were posted to the borough from 7th February, 1850.

Chapter Two

Violent times

Although crime had been reduced, these were still violent times for policemen. Newspapers regularly featured details of disturbances in which officers were injured. In 1857, PC Jonathon Bradley of Oldbury arrested labourer William Causer for being drunk and disorderly. The officer was attacked by one of the prisoner's friends, which enabled him to escape. A short time later the officer again arrested Causer and took him to the police station, where the prisoner produced a pair of scissors and stabbed the policeman several times. Causer was fined 10/- (50p) with costs. The policeman resigned the following year.

Another incident occurred in the same year at Stourbridge Road, Islington, near Halesowen, when PC Angus Kennedy was stoned by a gang of rowdy individuals whom he had asked to moderate their behaviour. The officer was struck many times, and at the later trial of one of the group, William Pritchard of Lye, he produced his badly battered hat for the magistrates to examine. Pritchard was fined 40/- (£2.00) with costs and sentenced to a month in prison if he failed to pay.

Within a few days of the Islington disturbance, PC Thomas Bradshaw of Dudley was on night duty in Bond Street when he saw a man named George Farmer fighting. The officer tried to intervene, but Farmer began to fight with him instead. They both fell over and Farmer was pulled into a nearby house by a friend. PC Bradshaw refused to release his prisoner and was beaten almost insensible. Fortunately, PC William Sier came to his assistance. He broke down the door to the house and tried to arrest Farmer. The officer was undeterred when the man threatened to "smash his head as flat as a penny", and chased him up a flight of stairs where he encountered three women who tried to prevent his progress. Eventually, with the aid of a member of the public, Farmer and his associate, Samuel Harris, were arrested. At a later court hearing, Farmer was sent to the House of Correction for two months' hard labour. Harris portrayed himself to the court as an innocent bystander, but he failed to convince the magistrates and was fined 80/- shillings (£4.00) with costs.

In June 1857, one policeman was assaulted and two were roughly handled when Macarte's Circus visited Malvern. Alfred Phipps, a carriage washer from the circus, was found fighting at the Lygon Arms. PC Benjamin Spiers tried to break up the fight and was assaulted by Phipps, who was subsequently arrested. Whilst he was in custody a gang of men attempted to release him. As a result, PCs Thomas Ludlow and William Stanton were knocked about and badly shaken before the escape bid was repelled. Later, at the magistrates court, Phipps was fined 10/- (50p) with 15/6d (77½p) costs or sentenced to an alternative of fourteen days' hard labour, in default.

At a public house in Cradley in 1863, PC Robert Woodward was attacked by John Robinson and his son-in-law. To prevent the officer from protecting himself, Robinson's daughters held onto his arms. The injuries he sustained meant that PC Woodward was unfit to work the following day.

PC Henry Pantin suffered even greater injuries when in January 1857, he was on patrol in Dudley at a place called Spring's Mire. As he passed an engine house, which should have been shut up, Pantin heard a noise and saw a light flashing inside. He knocked on the door and then tried to open it, but the door was secured from the inside. Suddenly the door opened and three men rushed out. One of them had an iron bar and he struck the officer with it, causing him to fall backwards off the steps leading up to the building. When Pantin hit the ground, all three men began to beat him, two with iron bars and one with a large spanner. Pantin managed to get one of the men under him and tried to keep him there, but his associates rescued him and they all ran away. Pantin struggled to a nearby house and, when he was examined by a doctor, it was found that he had ten separate wounds through his scalp to his skull and that one of his fingers was broken. Meanwhile, a search of the engine house found that the engine had been completely stripped of its brass parts, but they were left on the floor of the building. PC Pantin, however, was in a critical condition for some time. The attack left him severely disabled and he was retired from the force six months later on a pension of 12/6d (62½p) per week. His assailants were never found.

Unsatisfactory wages

A combination of the rigours of policing and the inadequate financial rewards resulted in a steady decline in recruiting. By 1847 it was proving extremely difficult to obtain candidates at all, and the quality of those applicants who did come forward was very disappointing. Sixteen shillings (80p) a week was just not enough to attract recruits of the right calibre. Wages outside the police force varied depending upon the occupation followed, but an average annual income at that time would have been at least £44.0.0d, compared with £41.12.0d (£41.60) received by policemen.

Negotiating wage settlements or improved conditions was out of the question for a policeman. There was no national bargaining mechanism, and complaining to a senior officer was frowned upon. The only way constables could express their views was to leave the service or transfer to a police force paying better wages. In some cases, life outside the force was no better and a few of the disgruntled men rejoined.

The seriousness of the situation caused the Court of Quarter Sessions to review its earlier decision to cut the wage bill. The basic weekly wage for a constable was increased by 1/- (5p), and the salary for other ranks by proportionate amounts. This increase in expenditure meant that savings had to be made elsewhere. To this end, the services of the weights and measures inspectors were dispensed with and their work was transferred, as additional duties, to police officers.

Poor accommodation

The living conditions for policemen varied greatly. In many cases it is likely that the housing was no worse than that endured by the working class of the time, but nevertheless, the consequences of living in a poor environment became tragedies for some families.

At Stourbridge police station the privies drained into a well in the small back yard. Charlotte Burton, the superintendent's wife succumbed to fever in October 1847, whilst their children suffered severe illness, but fortunately recovered. Although the surgeon who had attended the family had repeatedly told Henry Burton not to live at the police station because of the insanitary conditions, which were the cause of the fever, Burton would not heed the warnings. Matters did not improve for Burton when he moved to take charge of the Dudley division in 1857. He and his family once again suffered the consequences of unhealthy accommodation and poor sanitary conditions. The local magistrates reported to the Quarter Sessions that the Burton family was ill from the moment they took up residence at the police station.

At Stourport the police station was leased from the Staffordshire and Worcestershire Canal Company. The Company, with apparent disregard for residents in the vicinity, dredged the canal bed and then raised the level of water in the basin by about twelve inches (30cms). This caused drains carrying refuse water from the police station to back up, with a consequential accumulation of filth and dampness. Representations were made to the canal company, who responded by lowering the water level. Unfortunately the problem did not go away, and the stench that had been created, combined with the smells emanating from some of the persons detained in the cells, often filled the living quarters occupied by Superintendent John Bevan and his family.

A local builder examined the premises in 1850 and reported the conditions to be so bad that the Chief Constable paid a visit to see the situation for himself. He found that the stables had become flooded, making it necessary to raise the floor. Prisoners in the cells became so wet when detained overnight that it was necessary to dry their clothes in front of a fire. Many of the prisoners suffered sore throats and hoarseness. One of them, Eliza Peters, lost her voice completely. To treat her condition, leeches were applied to her throat when she arrived at the hospital in the county gaol. The accommodation difficulties were finally resolved when Edward Ingram, a local solicitor and Clerk to the Magistrates, offered alternative premises in York Street. These premises were refurbished and provided rooms for the superintendent and a constable, along with their families, together with three cells, a stable and coachhouse.

When Superintendent Bevan and his family moved to Bromsgrove they were no better off. The police station was an extremely unhealthy place to live in. Two of his children died having been exposed to the surroundings. "...there was an entire absence of all drainage in the original construction, thus rendering the house damp and unhealthy from foul air with reservoirs of blood for pigs on the other side of the contiguous road…there were open privies and cesspools on the opposite side of the road…" said a report to the police committee.

Many of the main police stations were cramped and totally inadequate for their purpose. Witley police station was a typical example. It comprised two cottages in which rooms on one side were used as a charge room and cells, and, on the other, as living quarters for Superintendent William Forty and PC George Attwood, and their families. The carthouse and the stabling for the horse were half a mile away at the Hundred House hotel. At Wolverley the station was occupied by Sergeant John Turner. When prisoners were taken into custody, they had to pass through part of his living quarters to be placed in a cell.

All over the county the police authority was faced with similar stories, each demanding priority. Although the ambitious programme of building, refurbishing or replacing continued the whole process became a never-ending cycle.

Superannuation scheme

Financing any of these projects was always difficult and the police committee had to look at a variety of proposals designed to raise funds. In 1841 the force introduced a superannuation scheme that allowed officers to make weekly contributions to provide pensions and lump sums for retiring and incapacitated colleagues. Certain fines and fees from the courts were added to the fund, as well as fines imposed upon policemen for disciplinary matters. It became routine for the authority to take loans from this account to pay for the building projects, and whilst this was not illegal, it certainly had a disastrous effect on the capital in the fund.

The Court of Quarter Sessions held the purse strings to the superannuation fund. Those police officers who were injured or disabled whilst on duty and unable to continue became the recipients of generous financial handouts. An example was PC Richard Brecknell who had joined the force in 1847 at the age of thirty-six. In less than two years his leg was broken whilst on duty and he had to leave the force. Brecknell was a tailor by trade and intended to return to his former occupation. He was discharged with a gratuity of £50.00d, which represented a great many contributions by his colleagues.

This combination of loans and liberal gratuities could not be sustained, time and again the pension scheme was short of funds. Applications by the chief constable for the Court of Quarter Sessions to direct more fines and fees into the fund's coffers were a regular feature of the minutes of the quarterly meetings.

Working conditions

It was against this background that the Victorian policeman worked in conditions that were considerably less than perfect, even for the nineteenth century. He had no time set aside for his refreshment break and worked every day of every week without respite. It was not until the 1860s that some days off were allowed; even then they were irregular and could not be counted on as an entitlement.

The county policeman could be posted anywhere in Worcestershire, and the contrast between urban and rural could not have been more marked. The tranquil and rustic nature of the Vale of Evesham, Malvern, Redditch and Tenbury, all situated in the south was so very different from the industrial north, which included Dudley, Halesowen, Oldbury and Lye, known collectively as part of the Black Country. In 1850 the Scots writer Dr Samuel Smiles described the Black Country as a place where "The earth seems to have been turned inside out. Its entrails are strewn about… the surface of the ground is covered with cinder heaps and coal is blazing on the surface." At night, he said, "The country is glowing with fire and the smoke hovers over it." There was indeed a constant stench as the fumes from the foundries lay on the air. Certainly, it was a place that took some getting used to, particularly for a bobby brought up in the country.

Conference points

In the 1850s, the establishment of a system of conference points enabled constables on adjoining beats, or even from adjacent forces, to meet up and pass on information, letters and other correspondence. These points would normally be at the boundaries of two beats, such as a crossroads in rural districts, or a shop or factory in a town area. It would be a regular meeting spot that enabled colleagues and supervising officers to know where the men could be contacted at a predetermined time. The arrangement was also a safety measure, because officers who did not 'make a point' would be quickly missed and searched for. A constable who failed to make a point without good cause could expect severe punishment.

Rewards for good work

The demanding work of the policemen was recognised very early on when the police authority introduced a reward scheme. A good arrest or a brave act by an officer, accompanied by a chief constable's recommendation, could trigger a cash payment. Normally it was no more than a pound or two, but nevertheless very welcome to those men who earned less than that in a week.

In 1851, Superintendent William Harris was an early beneficiary of the reward scheme. He was stationed at Pershore and lived at the police station in Bridge Street. One day he saw two scruffy men riding horses past the station. Neither of the men appeared to have the means to own a horse, so Harris and a constable set off in pursuit. They caught up with the men at Allesborough Hill, about a mile from the town centre. The two men did not give a good account of themselves, and the policemen engaged the assistance of a Mr Jeremy, of the Plough Inn at Pershore to arrest them. It turned out that the horses had been stolen the day before from Enstone, near Chipping Norton in Oxfordshire. Both men were later transported for seven years.

Another superintendent, John Bevan from Bromsgrove, was handsomely rewarded with the sum of £14.5.0d (£14.25) for his work in the investigation of a series of fires at Inkberrow in 1857. For several weeks the lives of many people in the village were severely disrupted, as they suffered the attentions of at least one arsonist who caused thousands of pounds worth of damage. Hay and straw ricks were set ablaze as well as sheds and farm outbuildings. The first fire occurred when a barley rick belonging to a Miss Rand was set on fire. Although the Feckenham and Alcester fire engines were quickly on the scene, the barley rick and two hay ricks were destroyed. The police quickly arrested labourer and local criminal James Hall. Less than two weeks later there was a fire at a farm near Inkberrow vicarage. This time there was not a lot of damage, but a thatcher named Henry Harris, who was an associate of James Hall, had been seen in the farmyard shortly before the fire started. He was arrested and found to have sufficient matches in his possession to get him remanded in custody.

Police activity in and around Inkberrow became intense, with policemen brought into the area from all parts of the county. They were instructed to patrol through farmyards, into fields, wherever there were hay and straw ricks. A reward of £30 offered by the village, with a similar sum put up by the Home Office, failed to produce information, and the fires continued. The influence of local landowner and Member of Parliament, W Laslett Esq., led to the Norwich Union fire engine 'Niagara', being stationed in the village.

On 4th December 1857, the fires ceased suddenly when nineteen-year-old Inkberrow farmer's son, William Davis, was arrested at the scene of a fire near to the Inkberrow churchyard. The Himbleton policeman John Leech saw the fire and rushed to the scene. He found Davis behind the burning rick. Davis claimed that he had seen the fire from his home, but at his trial this was shown to have been impossible. Nevertheless, the prosecution case became weakened when the investigation procedures were scrutinised, and this led to Davis' acquittal. The first two suspects were never tried.

An error of judgement

In the same year as the fires, problems over the county boundaries surfaced. The difficulties were such that it was virtually impossible for the police committee to decide where proposed police stations should be built in some parts of the county.

When the Worcestershire Constabulary was first formed in 1839 it policed all of the county along with detached parts of other counties, of which Halesowen and Oldbury were good examples. Legislation known as Scott's Act was introduced in 1844 and was designed to settle these boundary irregularities. Unfortunately the legislation was open to more than one interpretation, and by 1857 there were pressures on Worcestershire to allow Staffordshire to take control of Dudley and Oldbury, whilst Warwickshire was calling for Shipston on Stour, Yardley and Oldberrow to be merged into that county.

To deal with the inconsistencies that had been raised, Parliament introduced the County Bill. It was not controversial and was to pass through the Houses quickly. Members for Staffordshire had voiced certain reservations but their concerns had been resolved. One of the main outcomes of the proposed legislation in Worcestershire was that Dudley would become part of Staffordshire.

On 5th August 1857, the day before the Bill was due for its third and final reading, the chief constable, Richard Harris, and the mayor of Dudley, John Renand, went to London. They gained an interview with the Home Secretary, Sir George Grey, and voiced their concerns about the Bill. The next day they had a meeting with local MP and chairman of the police committee, Sir John Pakington. Harris once again expressed his disquiet about the Bill. He spoke of the considerable inconvenience for policemen who were required to attend trials in Worcester, if Dudley went into Staffordshire. He also felt that those men who transferred from Worcestershire to Staffordshire would lose the benefit of their former service towards their superannuation.

The mayor of Dudley, on the other hand, seemed to be totally confused by it all. He produced a petition containing twenty or thirty signatures from people who felt that the Bill would "injuriously affect the interests of Dudley". When Pakington pressed the mayor about his views, Renand said he did not understand the subject. The MP spent some time explaining and reassuring both men that their concerns were unfounded and then went to vote on the Bill. It was too late. The chief constable's protestations had caused Sir George Grey to have second thoughts about pressing on and the Bill was abandoned.

When the police committee met on Wednesday 12th August 1857, there was considerable anger and hostility directed towards the chief constable in the aftermath of the now defunct Bill. The committee's plans for an increase in the number of policemen and the building of new police stations were put on one side whilst an investigation was carried out into Harris' behaviour.

At a special police committee meeting on 12th September, Sir John Pakington reported, in the presence of the chief constable, the events leading to the termination of the County Bill. The committee decided that a report would be submitted to the next Court of Quarter Sessions expressing their dissatisfaction with Harris and stating that he had lost their confidence.

In a sombre atmosphere the report was presented to the Michaelmas Sessions. It recognised Harris' long service, but questioned whether in the light of events he could now retain his office. Harris spoke for himself at the hearing and, in a prepared statement, he told the court that he had agreed to meet urgently in London with the mayor of Dudley, to make representations about the Bill. As time was pressing he did not have the opportunity to advise the police committee of his actions, but he acknowledged that this was an "indiscretion". He went on to say that he was unable to get a meeting with Sir John Pakington at the House of Commons, and so, with the Bill due for its third reading the following day, he and the mayor approached the Home Secretary personally to express their concerns.

Harris expressed his "deep regret" to Pakington, the police committee and the Court of Quarter Sessions, and continued, "I earnestly hope... the court will bear in mind that I originally formed and organised the police force in 1839... and served the county in the capacity of chief constable without impeachment." He described his actions as "more an error of judgement than wilful dereliction of duty."

As Harris placed himself at the mercy of the court, there were many members present who felt that it was inconceivable that he should retain his position as head of the police force. However, in the ensuing ballot there were thirty-four votes supporting his dismissal and thirty-eight accepting his apology and favouring his retention. The effects of Harris' misguided behaviour dogged him for the rest of his service. Many magistrates neither forgot nor forgave him for his inept behaviour.

First government inspection

The introduction of the County and Borough Police Act in 1856 gave the government the opportunity to assess the efficiency of police forces. Government Inspectors were appointed to carry out annual inspections, which, if favourable, would lead to that force receiving a government grant.

Her Majesty's Inspector of Constabulary (HMI), Major General William Cartwright, made his first visit to Worcestershire on 16th December 1856, and soon realised that the force was under strength. He recommended that the police committee increase the number of men by twenty-seven. To show government support for Cartwright, the Home Office quickly approved an increase in the force establishment by a similar figure. The committee chose to ignore the connection and implemented only part of Cartwright's recommendations by increasing the number of constables in some areas of the county, but not others.

In a subsequent visit, Cartwright proposed changes in the salary structure. He also observed that many of the cells in the county were unfit for their role. Some contained open fires, whilst many of them were constructed in such a way that prisoners were unable to get the attention of the policeman responsible for looking after them.

Harris tried hard to encourage the committee to carry out another recommendation made by Cartwright. It was for a rolling reserve of eight constables, to be held in training at headquarters. The chief constable's application reflected his concern at the difficulties he had encountered in keeping the peace at recent disturbances at Oldbury. A strike by colliers in 1858, had required him to deploy almost half of his men to the area for three months. With no reserves to fall back on, substantial sections of the county had been left without police cover. He had moved the men to Oldbury at the request of the local magistrates, and the police committee had not been consulted. Its members subjected Harris to a collective sulk peppered with advice that benefited from an ample measure of hindsight, showing that the committee was prepared to try and influence the chief constable in policing matters whenever it was so inclined.

The first detective

In his quest to increase the number of policemen under his command, Harris held a long-standing desire to employ detectives. He had started his crusade in 1850 but the police committee did not share his enthusiasm. Although his presentation of the request to the committee proved to be amateurish and clumsy, greater influences were at work. There was a general fear across the country that policemen operating in plain clothes were a threat to liberty, and that a secret organisation spying upon British citizens would develop.

In 1857, Harris, possibly without the knowledge of the police committee, took some cautious steps in this direction by appointing Detective Sergeant George Davies at Dudley. Davies joined the force on 1st May at the age of thirty-nine, and although he must have had previous police experience, no details remain. Within a few months of joining, Davies was sent to assist in the investigations into the farm fires at Inkberrow, but it was another two years before he was officially mentioned in police records as a detective and paid a plain-clothes allowance.

What was expected of Davies as a detective is not clear, but it could have included the service of summonses and legal documents. One report shows him on duty in plain-clothes in New Street, Dudley, at about 11.00p.m. A woman named Mary Wilson, accompanied by two men, approached him and took his arm. At the same time she asked him for money to buy porter and began patting his trouser pockets as if searching for money. What Mary had to say when she was let into the sergeant's secret is not recorded, but her misbehaviour earned her a month in prison with hard labour.

Chapter Three

The railway

The development of the railway in the county brought with it a fresh dimension to police work. Not only was it necessary to deal with the problems created by communities of construction workers, but also to confront the crime that accompanied this new transport system.

In 1857 the chief constable was asked to supply constables to the railway companies, as and when required, at their expense. This was not an unusual request as, for some time, extra constables had been recruited for private employers. Three years later the force began to recruit officers specifically as railway policemen, as in the case of PC William Broadhurst and PC John Rose, who both served at Shrub Hill railway station. They soon resigned, probably as a consequence of the wages, which were always at the bottom of the pay scale.

Low pay may have led to the downfall of PC Thomas Martin, who was stationed at Malvern railway station on the Great Western Railway. He joined the constabulary on 20th August 1863, aged twenty-five. He was formerly a clerk and a native of Matlock in Derbyshire. Contemporary newspaper reports describe him as a "cab inspector, occasionally employed as a policeman." On Monday 18th January 1864, he appeared before Malvern magistrates charged with entering the Malvern station booking office, where he forced a drawer and stole 12/6d (62½p). He was dismissed from the police force and sentenced to five years' penal servitude.

The arrangement to supply constables to the railway companies came to rather an abrupt end in January 1865, when PC William Reeve, the last of twenty-six railway policemen, left Shrub Hill. The removal of PC Reeve may have coincided with the withdrawal, in December 1864, of a courtesy extended by the railway authorities to the chief constable, allowing him to travel on their trains free of charge.

An increase in responsibilities

Although the county constabulary had been in existence for little more than twenty years, many local authorities soon realised that some of their responsibilities could be offloaded onto the police. It might be said that some of the work could benefit police intelligence, but the duties were unpaid and often consumed a considerable, disproportionate amount of police time. In Malvern, for example, the police were responsible for the relief of vagrants. The residents of the town were encouraged to refer all beggars to the local police office, to enable an investigation into their means to take place. And so it went on. Policemen became inspectors of common lodging houses and assistant surveyors of parish roads, to name just two. The crunch came in 1865 when the Redditch authorities appointed three local policemen as inspectors of public nuisances. Within four months, Superintendent John Bevan was complaining that these men were spending more time dealing with their ancillary tasks than with their police work. Bevan's grievance led the Court of Quarter Sessions to instruct that police officers would no longer be appointed to these secondary duties. In reality it took more than a hundred years for the practice to cease.

A question of judgement

The work of a police officer requires a large measure of judgement. The line between acting and not acting is often a narrow one. Whatever decision is made, there is always the possibility that the response will be clinically scrutinised, usually in an entirely different environment to that in which the incident in question arose.

On 24th November 1860, PC Philip Randall of Longdon police station was on duty at Heath Hill, Ripple, when he saw William Tandy, a crippled sixteen-year-old, standing in a field holding a gun, occasionally aiming the weapon at imaginary targets, but not firing. The officer approached the boy, who was walking with the aid of a crutch. During the course of their conversation the boy told the policeman that he had the gun with him to frighten birds off his master's crops. Randall decided to check the lad's story with the landowner, who asked the officer to return to the field and take the gun, powder and shot from the boy. When the policemen spoke to the boy an argument developed between them, which resulted in Tandy holding the gun barrel to the constable's cheek. As Randall pushed the gun away from him, it discharged and a violent struggle took place before Tandy was overpowered. The case against William Tandy was heard by Judge Baron Wilde at Worcester Assizes. During the case, the officer was castigated by both defending counsel and the judge, for "grossly exceeding his duty" and "acting more as a gamekeeper than a policeman".

In another firearm incident, on Sunday 6th March 1864, PC John Lane of Elmley Castle came across labourer George Fletcher at Netherton, near Pershore. It was about 5.00p.m in the evening and the officer could see that Fletcher's coat pocket was bulging. The officer asked him what was in it, but the replies were unhelpful. The policeman tried to search the man, but was prevented from doing so and punched several times. It transpired that Fletcher was carrying a loaded gun in a number of pieces, and Lane had to "nearly strangle" the man before he would release it. At Pershore petty sessions, two days later, Fletcher claimed to be acting in self-defence when he assaulted the policeman, but the magistrates conferred briefly and found him guilty. The case attracted considerable local interest, and when the public watching the proceedings heard the result they became very agitated and expressed their disgust at the verdict. The defendant was fined 1/- (5p) with 7/6d (37½p) costs or sentenced to fourteen days' hard labour. Fletcher paid up straight away.

One weapon in the armoury of a police officer is good observation accompanied by the ability to distinguish the normal from the untoward. In 1865 Sergeant Thomas Rowley thought something was amiss when he saw a well known poacher, John Leyster, carrying a "very fine berried holly" at Rowney Green near Alvechurch. Although Leyster had thought up a good excuse for possessing the holly, he was arrested. The following day, a Mr Twigg of Rowney Green reported that the top had been cut out of a holly tree in his garden. Sergeant Rowley was able to match Leyster's holly to Mr Twigg's tree, which resulted in Leyster being fined £2.0.0d, including costs.

A new uniform design

In the 1860s the uniform for a policeman began to change. Out went the swallow tail coat and the stovepipe hat. In came new caps, helmets and a frock coat buttoned to the waist. For the first time, a metal plate embossed with the county arms was introduced to be worn on the front of the helmets. The upright collars of the new coats still retained the officer's number and the county arms, but were far more comfortable to wear at the neck than the clothing they replaced. The broad leather belt continued to be worn and uniform trousers remained much the same, but were not pressed. Shoes and boots were often left dirty, with bumps and scuffs untouched. William Thomas, a shoemaker from Worcester, was contracted to supply two pairs of shoes for each constable, at a cost of 11/- (55p) a pair.

PC William Beavan c1905
A rare photograph of a Worcestershire policeman wearing
Foreign Legion style headgear with his summer uniform

Uniforms for the county policemen were not made to measure, except in the case of the chief constable, who received his first uniform in 1867. Whenever an officer left the force his uniform was returned to stores to await re-issue to a new recruit. To the storeman, the size of the recruit and the size of the uniform need not correspond. Indeed, a local tailor obtained much of his business from recruits who had to have their uniforms altered. The issue of second-hand uniform to recruits continued well into the 1970s. By this time more attention was given to sizings, and made-to-measure uniform was issued each year. When a constable left the force, he was expected to hand in a clean, complete and undamaged set of clothing. If he didn't, an appropriate sum was stopped from his final wage for cleaning, repair or replacement.

A patrolling policeman often carried a walking cane, and it was not unknown for miscreants to receive a sharp prod or stroke from it, when the officer felt such action was warranted. Generally such random discipline was accepted by the public, but should a complaint be received and substantiated, then the constable was in trouble. The cane was never officially part of a policeman's equipment, but officers continued to carry them well into the twentieth century.

Public appreciation

In many areas of the force, the policeman established himself as a highly respected and important member of the community. When it was time for him to move on, it was not unusual for local people to make a collection of money, and sometimes provide a gift, for the officer. At least two policemen who served at Bishampton benefited from such kind thoughts. PC George Edwards was given a purse of money and an inscribed watch in 1859, whilst PC Thomas Staite received a purse of money and a medal eleven years later. When Superintendent Henry Burton moved from Stourbridge to Dudley in 1857, he was given a silver cigar case in a morocco leather case. He was also presented with an inscribed and framed memorial.

Such presentations became a thing of the past when, in later years, the chief constable instructed that such gifts should not be accepted.

Mundane duties

Being a Victorian policemen brought with it few perks and pleasures. A constable posted to a town such as Redditch or Oldbury would find that his duties included the often unsavoury tasks of cleaning out the cells and emptying the soil buckets. He also had to keep the station fire well stoked up, with the ashes cleared away, as well as a multitude of other housekeeping duties. If he happened to be the superintendent's orderly, then he was regarded as a servant, whose duties included cleaning the senior officer's boots and preparing his uniform. He would also feed and groom the superintendent's horse, polish the police cart, and clean the tack making sure it was in good repair. On the positive side, the groom would be relieved of some of the mundane duties of his colleagues, often travelling further afield with his superintendent. In the case of Superintendent Jeffrey of Bromsgrove, in his later life he was often seen riding his horse, which was being led by his groom, PC Garfield Beesley.

Working at headquarters was no cushy number either. For many years John Oliver was stationed there as a clerk. His spidery script appears on many of the force's old documents. In 1871 Oliver made a list of the duties he carried out as a sergeant at Worcester. The contents ran to more than a page. He described his skills as those of an accountant, statistician, clerk, secretary, wages clerk, storeman, postal clerk and stationery clerk. He was also a station sergeant, patrolling policeman and a nanny to new recruits. In a final flourish he rounded off his job description with "…to make myself as useful as possible." John Oliver died in 1891. He was still an admin man and had risen through the ranks to become superintendent/chief clerk.

William Jeffrey
Superintendent at Bromsgrove
1879 - 1902

Retirement of the first chief constable and his deputy

On 2nd January 1871 the police committee reported the intended resignation of the chief constable to the Worcestershire Court of Quarter Sessions in the following terms: "Your committee have received a communication from Chief Constable Harris resigning his appointment on medical certificate, that he is no longer fitted to fulfil the arduous duties of his office. Setting out his long period of service in the county, now over thirty years and praying for the liberal consideration of the magistrates in awarding him a pension." The committee recommended that he receive a pension of £250 p.a. and that his resignation take effect on 3rd April 1871.

The police committee was ordered to advertise for candidates for the office of chief constable, and to submit not less than three names of applicants for the decision of the court.

In this very businesslike fashion, the career of Richard Reader Harris, for more than thirty-one years the chief constable of Worcestershire, was brought to a close. There were no long speeches describing his loyalty, or the sadness that was felt at losing his services. Neither were there warm expressions of good wishes in his retirement. Rather, an unemotional acceptance of his departure.

Six months later the deputy chief constable retired. On this occasion the committee advised the Quarter Sessions, "Your committee have with regret to announce to the Court the retirement of Mr Richard James Lloyd the deputy chief constable. A faithful and efficient officer of thirty years standing. He having been appointed superintendent of police in the year of 1841 and deputy chief constable in 1845 and who now finds himself, from declining health and strength, unequal to the performance of the duties of his office. He has during this long period of service subscribed £100.12.6d (£100.62½) to the superannuation fund and your committee recommend that the full retiring allowance, namely two thirds of his present salary or £120 p.a. be granted to him…"

It is a sad reflection on the members of the police committee that they could not be as generous in their praise of Harris as they were of Richard Lloyd. As chief constable he had set up the force from scratch and managed it through some very difficult times. True, he had had his foolish moments, but he was treading new ground and should have been given credit for it. But, Harris did not fit in. He was not a member of the upper classes and the county elite. The authorities would not make the same mistake again.

Richard Reader Harris died alone in Bournemouth on 14th January 1892, at the age of eighty-three. He warranted little more than a single line obituary in local newspapers.

Part II

Chapter Four

A new leader

During the thirty or so years that had passed since the formation of the Worcestershire Constabulary, the force had more than quadrupled in size to 187 men. This growth was set to continue by 245% until 1911, a larger increase than any other county force in the same period.

Lt. Col. George Lyndock Carmichael
Chief Constable of the Worcestershire Constabulary
1871 - 1903

To lead the constabulary into the twentieth century, the Court of Quarter Sessions selected Lieutenant Colonel George Lyndoch Carmichael from a list of 121 applicants. He took up the post of chief constable on 3rd April 1871. The vacancy for the deputy chief constable was filled by Superintendent James Phillips, who was already in charge of the Worcester division based at the Loves Grove headquarters.

Although he lacked any police experience, Colonel Carmichael's military career was a distinguished one. Born in 1832, the son of David S. Carmichael-Smyth, a judge in the Supreme Court of Calcutta, Carmichael had the family credentials that Harris lacked. He was a married man and had a son, who was born at about the time of his appointment as chief constable. Carmichael was commissioned into the Derbyshire Regiment as an ensign in 1848, and four years later was promoted to lieutenant. He saw action at the Crimea in 1854 and fought with distinction in the Battles of Alma and Inkerman and at the siege and assaults on Sebastopol. In 1857 he went to India and served in Rajpootana and Central India during the Indian Mutiny. His service elsewhere in India resulted in a mention in despatches when he was granted the brevet rank of major on 15th November 1859. Colonel Carmichael retired from army service in February 1870, at the brevet rank of lieutenant colonel.

Carmichael quickly gained a reputation as a strict disciplinarian and does not appear to have suffered any obvious difficulties from not having the benefit of a police background.

Problem policemen

One of the first major internal problems to face Carmichael occurred at Halesowen in 1872, when an audit of the police accounts there revealed many discrepancies. The discovery was followed by the sudden disappearance of the local superintendent, Miles Overend, and his family. It transpired that a junior clerk from the magistrates clerk's office had been given the responsibility for checking the Halesowen police accounts. The clerk to the justices' did not supervise his work, and so irregularities going back more than two years, had lain undiscovered. Overend was never traced, and he may have returned to his native Ireland.

Miles Overend was not the only officer to flee from the force. At least fourteen other policemen absconded prior to 1905, including PC Henry Brereton, who was imprisoned for absconding in 1866.

Many more policemen were punished for being absent without leave. An officer could not leave his station, even when off duty, without written permission from his superintendent. This instruction was enforced well into the twentieth century. In 1928, PC John Whitmore, who was a single man, was dismissed after he spent two nights away from his quarters at Oldbury without permission.

When dealing with disciplinary matters, successive chief constables have, not unreasonably, placed a great deal of importance on honesty. Officers who were frank about their misdeeds often escaped severe punishment for comparatively serious misdemeanours. Those who were caught out being untruthful soon received their marching orders. A good example was PC Stephen Warmington. He was sacked in

1879 when it was discovered that he had failed to declare that he had been dismissed from the Hereford City police prior to joining the Worcestershire Constabulary.

Recruiting and training

The Warmington incident highlighted the shortcomings of the recruiting procedures being operated at that time. It is one of a number of examples where the doubtful background of a new policeman caught up with him. New candidates to the force were taken on as soon as they applied, and enquiries about their histories were made at a later stage. It could take two or three weeks, sometimes more, before a recruit's past was established. By the early part of the twentieth century the problem was eliminated, when all enquiries were made before applicants were accepted into the service. However, it was in the face of a deteriorating recruiting situation that some standards were completely overlooked. Health and education seem to be areas particularly neglected. A few men lasted only days before leaving because of ill health. The education of some recruits was described as 'imperfect', 'poor', 'fair', and 'very fair', although it is not clear against which set of standards these judgements were being measured. The ages of the men accepted into the force also varied considerably. For example, PC Charles Stanford from Sheriffs Lench and PC Oliver Morris from Feckenham were both seventeen when they joined, whilst at the other end of the scale PC Isaac Purcer joined in 1844 at the age of forty-eight. The force regarded the army as a rich source of potential recruits, and ex-guardsmen were particularly sought out. Nevertheless, the rapid turnover of men, through resignation or dismissal, ensured that the recruiting task was endless.

As soon as they were accepted into the force, the details of each recruit were entered onto large pre-printed forms, which were later bound into a ledger. The personal description of each man included height, weight, chest measurement, hat size, complexion, and eye and hair colouring. It was customary for the officer who completed the record to choose the colour of the recruit's eyes and hair, and, as a result, all recruits had grey or brown eyes with light, dark or brown hair. When PC William Rudd from Tenbury joined in 1883 he had the temerity to suggest that his eyes were blue. The entry on his record shows that his eyes were grey, followed by "(calls them blue)". It took until 1893 for the police force to acknowledge that some of its recruits had blue eyes.

As fresh trainees were taken on they were retained at headquarters as the 'reserve' that Richard Reader Harris had striven so hard to set up years before. Their time at Loves Grove was intended to be a training period, but some of their duties seemed quite inappropriate. They were expected to carry out general cleaning and polishing duties, as well as cutting buttons, which had some value, from old uniforms. Often they would be sent off, alone and on foot, in full uniform, to deliver messages to outstations on the outskirts of Worcester. Their remaining spare time was taken up with trying to learn the rudiments of their new career, punctuated with periods of drill and foot patrol, either alone or with an experienced officer. Their stay at headquarters could be anything from two to more than ninety days, but, at an average of forty-two days, they were unlikely to have been adequately prepared for what faced them.

Often these policemen were left to set their own standards of behaviour and could not fail to be influenced, to some degree, by life around them and the background they had been drawn from. Many of the people that they dealt with were chronic alcoholics, others were prostitutes and some were both. It is no surprise, therefore, that some police officers chose to take advantage of offers of drink and, in some cases, sexual favours. Even if these men did not find themselves compromised by their actions, the consequences often led to drunkenness, alcoholism, debt, ill health and, sooner or later, dismissal.

PC George Mantle from Mamble joined the force in January 1878, at the age of twenty-eight. The description contained in his personal record, creates a picture, in the mind's eye, of a man whose rosy countenance was due to an over exposure, to the extremes of weather, as a farm labourer. Unfortunately, his subsequent behaviour leads one to conclude that it was due to excesses of a different kind. Whilst at Broadwaters he was disciplined and fined 12/- (60p) for fighting whilst under the influence of drink. Within a short time he assaulted a Mr Adkins of Mill Street, Kidderminster, who was riding his bicycle through Broadwaters one evening. Mantle struck Adkins on the arm and drunkenly shouted, "What the b....y hell are you whistling at!" The local superintendent described Mantle as useless and recommended that he should go, which is what happened in 1879. In the same year, Redditch policeman PC Edward Hudspith was missing from his beat for four hours, and, when found, was 'helplessly drunk' and begging for money to buy more drink. He cursed loudly at passers-by who refused. Sensibly, Hudspith resigned before he could be sacked.

Society for the Prevention of Cruelty to Animals (SPCA)

In March 1877, PC J Doorbar was appointed as an additional constable to work for the Stourbridge branch of the SPCA. Doorbar was the first of a number of policemen employed at the SPCA's expense. Whilst the employment of policemen by local businesses was not unusual, for some reason the SPCA officers were treated differently in that they were never issued with a collar number. In fact, their standing in the force must have been extremely low. They were often left out of the monthly disposition list submitted to headquarters by the Stourbridge division, which was the only division from which they worked. The appointment of policemen as SPCA officers ended with Additional Constable James Brown. He had been called to give evidence in a case of cruelty to a horse, which was being heard at Kidderminster borough court. As the hearing progressed, it became apparent that Brown was giving untruthful and contradictory evidence that favoured the defendant. At the conclusion of the case, he was seen drinking in local pubs with the owner of the horse. This unacceptable conduct led to his dismissal.

The Blockley riot

The Blockley district is a largely rural area, but for a good part of the nineteenth century a number of silk mills offered employment in the village. As these mills began to close, jobs in the locality became scarce. Farmers were also feeling the pinch because of cheap grain imports from the United States, and the health of the community had taken a battering following an outbreak of small-pox. It was against this background that some of the locals turned to poaching to supplement their meagre food resources. Not surprisingly they crossed swords with gamekeepers and policemen who were strict in their enforcement of the law.

The resident police sergeant was Charles Drury, a native of Bretforton, a village not too far away. He lived in a police cottage in Lower Street, Blockley with his wife Mary.

Charles Drury
Superintendent at Upton
1889 - 1893
Served as Constable and Sergeant at Blockley

An influential resident and business man, Richard Boswell Belcher, takes up the story in his autobiography. "Two innocent young men fled from the village and never returned because they had picked up a rabbit they had found in a snare. Another was arrested for picking three partridge eggs which had been placed on the bare ground by the keeper. Yet another who was charged with poaching was put to the expense of £8 for a lawyer and a cartload of witnesses to establish his innocence. Oliver Booker was stopped on his way home by a bough blown off a tree, which had obstructed the traffic for many days. He took the bough into his trap and openly put it into his garden. Our zealous policeman obtained a warrant and Booker was locked up in a police cell for two days and nights and then committed to Worcester Sessions, where he was acquitted."

Events were approaching a climax when, on a Friday in March 1878, Sergeant Drury attempted to arrest a Blockley man named Jones for an offence of assault involving a servant girl. As so often happens in these cases, the couple in question 'made up' before the policeman was able to deal with the offender, who fought strongly with Drury to avoid arrest. In the ensuing struggle, a crowd gathered and was amused to see the wanted man escape and the policeman suffer a black eye.

Whilst on duty the following evening, Drury paid a routine visit to the Crown public house in the village. It was a most inopportune moment to call in. Earlier that day he had been to Shipston on Stour magistrates court to give evidence against a number of local men. No doubt this was the topic of conversation in the pub and feelings were running high. The story goes, that as he appeared through the door he was jeered and ridiculed about his black eye, and then beer mugs were thrown at him. The sergeant beat a hasty retreat, but the incident was the signal for a mob to form and he was chased through the High Street into the churchyard. The crowd pursued him into Lower Street, where he got to the police station and locked the door. In what must have been a terrifying experience, his pursuers began to bombard the station with a variety of missiles before breaking in. Drury was dragged outside, being beaten about the head, and then stoned, kicked and trampled on. Some locals eventually came to his rescue and he was taken to a nearby house so that his wounds could be treated.

There were a number of villagers who took part in the riot and they were soon rounded up, however, some of the troublemakers were not local. They had been brought to the area to fell trees at nearby Springhill. These men were not traced.

Belcher became the self-appointed spokesman for the people of Blockley who believed that the real offenders had got away. He wrote to the *Evesham Journal* newspaper in June 1878 and was extremely critical of the police and their reactions towards the villagers after the riot. He accused policemen of using unnecessary force to prevent the loitering of persons in the streets. He called for enquiries into the operation of the Shipston magistrates court and asked why magistrates allowed a disproportionate number of public houses to operate in a village the size of Blockley, one so far off the beaten track. The letter struck a nerve at the Quarter Sessions, and members sought the advice of Counsel to establish whether it was libellous. Legal proceedings were not attempted, but there was a futile exchange of letters between Belcher and the clerk to the Court of Quarter Sessions before the matter was finally laid to rest. Meanwhile, extra police were drafted into Blockley until the police station had been repaired and fears of a further disturbance had subsided.

Sergeant Drury continued to work at Blockley until 1879. He later moved to Malvern where he became the superintendent.

Droitwich and Bewdley forces absorbed

At the beginning of the 1880s, the watch committees of the boroughs of Droitwich and Bewdley realised that they could not continue with their current policing arrangements. As early as 1857, the HMI, Major General Cartwright, had criticised Bewdley for employing two elderly, underpaid constables who were permitted to continue in their own businesses when not called upon to be policemen. Cartwright had also told Droitwich, on more than one occasion, that a sergeant and constable were insufficient to police the borough. Little had changed in the ensuing years.

Agreements were reached between the county and the borough authorities, which led to the county constabulary assuming the policing role. Droitwich was taken over on 1st August 1881, followed by Bewdley eight months later. Only John Colley, who was in charge of the Droitwich force, was retained. He served as a Sergeant at Droitwich for a short period before being posted to Broadwaters.

The murder of a policeman

In 1885 the only Worcestershire policeman to be murdered was found dead in a country lane near Redditch. Since that time there has been vigorous debate, both locally and further afield, as to the guilt of the man who was eventually convicted and hung for the offence.

PC James Davis
Photographed at Droitwich in February, 1885,
shortly before his murder

The policeman was James Davis, a former miner from Stourbridge. He was, at 5'7½", quite a short man, but of stocky build, sporting a full, bushy black beard. In 1874 he married Elizabeth Burness from Richmond in Surrey, and a year later joined the Kidderminster borough police force, where he served for three years. Following his discharge he started his own business, dealing in glass and china at Stourport. He gave up trading three years later and joined the Worcestershire Constabulary on 15th April 1880 at the age of twenty-eight. His first posting was Beoley, near Redditch.

At about 11.30p.m. on Friday 27th February 1885, PC Davis set out to patrol his beat on foot. He left his heavily pregnant wife and three children at their police cottage on the outskirts of the village. As with all local policemen of the time, he had a twenty-four-hour responsibility and would often make his rounds at irregular and unsociable hours.

The following morning, at about 8.30a.m., John Twigg, a farmer from Rowney Green, was on his way to work at Weatheroak Hill, when he came across a body in Eagle Street Lane (also known as Icknield Street), Weatheroak. The body was that of James Davis. He had been viciously mutilated with a knife and had suffered stab wounds about the head and throat. Whilst trying to defend himself, two fingers on his left hand and one on his right were almost severed. Mr Twigg reported what he had found to a nearby farm and the police were called. The body was then removed to the premises of a local wheelwright.

Superintendent William Jeffrey, from Bromsgrove, led the murder enquiries and set about tracing the route that PC Davis had taken that night. It was established that, at about 1.00a.m., he had met PC Frederick Whitehouse from Wythall. They conferred together in a shed near to the Rose and Crown pub. It may well have been that they were keeping observations for poachers. After about an hour they resumed patrol together until they got to Portway at about 2.15a.m. There they separated and went their own ways. Davis was due to meet PC Sheppard from Alvechurch, at Seecham near Rowney Green at about 4.00a.m., but Sheppard was sick and did not go on duty that night.

Local enquiries soon revealed that there had been a theft of poultry from a Weatheroak farm. The woodland near to where the body of the dead officer was found, was known to be a haunt for poachers and fowl stealers. The scene of the murder was carefully examined and it was obvious that there had been a violent struggle. There were chicken feathers everywhere and the policeman's whistle and an oak stick were found about two hundred yards from the body.

Superintendent Jeffrey's local knowledge, and marks found in the lane, led him to suspect that the offender was a known local poacher. He circulated the man's details, by telegraph, to surrounding police stations, and the enquiry was then taken up by Superintendent Alfred Tyler based at Kings Heath. Accompanied by officers from the Birmingham police, he went to a garret at 9 Bartholomew Street, Birmingham. There they found the suspect, Moses Shrimpton, in bed with Jane Morton, with whom he had been living for some time. Morton was forty years old and the wife of a Redditch bricklayer. She was known to use more than one name, and newspapers later described her as a prostitute.

**Moses Shrimpton in 1885
at the time of his conviction for the murder
of PC James Davis**

An examination of Shrimpton's clothes revealed that they were extensively bloodstained, although some effort had been made to clean them. A knife found in Morton's possession appeared to have been wiped by plunging the blade into the ground. Shrimpton exhibited signs of a recent head injury, which he attributed to a fall when he was drunk about a month before, then later claimed that it had happened the previous week. The wound was examined by a doctor, who found that it had been inflicted within the previous twenty-four hours by a blunt instrument. When PC Davis' staff was discovered, it was bloodstained and had hair on it.

As the investigation developed, it was revealed that the watch PC Davis usually carried with him was missing. Enquiries showed that Jane Morton had tried to sell or at least raise money against a watch. It was never established whether the watches were one and the same. Neither watch was traced and there is a suggestion that the watch in Morton's possession was thrown into a furnace to destroy it.

Moses Shrimpton was a man of about sixty-five, but similar in stature to James Davis. In spite of his age he was described as being a strong man who had operated outside the law for most of his life. His previous convictions ran well into double figures and he was no stranger to the inside of gaols. It was said that on more than one occasion he had taken steps to ensure that he had the benefit of a short sentence in gaol around Christmas time. Some newspapers described Shrimpton as a local man whilst others said he came from Buckinghamshire. He certainly had family links in Redditch and had worked as a needle maker at Hunt End, in his early life.

From Fruit Trees to Furnaces - A History of the Worcestershire Constabulary   43

PC Moses Haynes
Droitwich
February 1885

James Davis was not the first policeman to be injured by Shrimpton. In 1868 he had attacked PC Moses Haynes of Webheath. The incident arose when PC Haynes had occasion to seize a gun from Shrimpton. The officer locked the gun away at Redditch police station, and later the same day Shrimpton lay in wait for him to return home through Tilehouse Woods. As the officer passed by, Shrimpton struck, and began beating Haynes about the head with a gun barrel. The attack was so violent that passers-by had to help the officer to take the poacher into custody. The affair earned Shrimpton four years' penal servitude.

The funeral of James Davis took place at Beoley and the cortege included representatives from many of the surrounding police forces. The Birmingham police band played the "Dead March" from Handel's "Saul" as the procession followed the

> **In Affectionate Remembrance of**
> **JAMES DAVIS,**
> WHO WAS BRUTALLY MURDERED WHILE IN THE EXECUTION OF HIS DUTY ON FERRUARY 28TH, 1885,
> **AGED 34 YEARS.**
>
> A fond and loving husband who was killed in the prime of life,
> He little thought when he went out that night would be his last,
> Cursed was that cruel hand that caused the fatal wound,
> But now laid low to rest in peace in the silent tomb.

A black bordered remembrance card produced in 1885 to raise funds for the family of the murdered policeman James Davis. Unfortunately the month of his death was not spelled correctly.

coffin. The murder had moved many local people, who were eager to assist in any way they could, both at the funeral and by contributing to a fund set up for Mrs Davis and her children. The proceeds from the sale of black-bordered remembrance cards, printed in large numbers and sold for 6d (2½p) each, were also added to the fund. Money began to roll in from all over the country. The final tally was more than £1,400 which was supplemented by a gratuity of £60.16.8d (£60.82) from the police authority.

Moses Shrimpton was tried at Worcestershire Assizes. Counsel for the defence warned the jury against finding his client guilty solely upon circumstantial evidence, but the jury was convinced, and Shrimpton was convicted of the murder of James Davis. It was the practice to allow three Sundays to elapse between the passing of sentence and its implementation. On Monday 25th May 1885, at 8.00a.m., Shrimpton was executed.

The newspapers produced countless column inches on the whole affair. Some reporters were allowed to view the execution and a Redditch journalist graphically described how the noose tore at Shrimpton's neck, creating a spectacle similar to that of his victim as he lay dead in Eagle Street Lane.

The story does not end there. Thomas Bayliss, a local surveyor and inspector of nuisances, was employed to draw a plan of the murder scene. When he submitted his account for payment, the Court of Quarter Sessions considered it excessive and refused to authorise payment in full. There were murmurings of legal action to recover the outstanding balance of £30.1.7d (£30.08), but in the end the Court relented and agreed to clear the account completely.

The memory of PC James Davis lives on. His body was laid in Beoley churchyard and is still marked by a headstone. At the scene of his murder lies a simple stone inscribed 'J.D. 1885'.

Chapter Five

A new police authority

The process of the police becoming publicly accountable took a small step forward when the Local Government Act of 1888 arrived on the statute book. For the first time, elected councillors joined the magistrates on the police authority and overall responsibility for the police moved away from the Court of Quarter Sessions to the Worcestershire County Council.

The police authority in its fresh guise and with a new title, the Standing Joint Committee (SJC), met for the first time on Saturday 13th April 1889, at 11.30a.m., under the chairmanship of W. George Woodyatt MP.

An embarrassing affair

The change in the constitution of the police authority did little to help the force when it was rocked by a scandal. Press interest in the incident ensured that the authorities rapidly lost control of the war of words, in the face of a concerted campaign of support for a police officer who was perceived to have been wronged by 'the system'. The unwritten doctrine of the police force to resist, at all costs, any attempt to have its dirty linen washed in public resulted in it having a severe mauling in newsprint.

The incident which triggered the press attention occurred at Pershore in 1892 and the story contains enough intrigue to become a novel in its own right. The policeman in question, Superintendent Henry Kemp, was alleged to have behaved in a manner which breached Victorian moral principles, just when they were at their strongest. Kemp had been a superintendent for almost twenty years, serving at Halesowen before taking charge at Pershore in May, 1881. He was a married man with seven children.

Born in Leicester, he had worked as a warehouseman before joining the Birmingham borough police force in 1864 at the age of twenty-three, serving at Staniforth Street. In February 1868, apparently at the request of the chief constable, Richard Harris, he transferred to Worcestershire, to deal with a crime wave at Balsall Heath. He was immediately appointed as a detective sergeant and served at Balsall Heath for nine months. He later moved to Ombersley, Bromsgrove, Redditch, Broadwas, and again to Ombersley. In 1872 he was posted to Halesowen as a newly promoted superintendent.

In January 1883, Kemp, together with William Hinton, an Inland Revenue officer, was awarded the Albert Medal in Bronze for gallantry, following an incident in 1881. They had both entered a burning ironmongers store at Halesowen and removed canisters of gunpowder and blasting powder. Rumours circulating at the time suggested Kemp had accepted the award when it should have gone to a constable who was at the scene.

Henry Kemp
Superintendent at Pershore
1881 - 1892
wearing his Albert Medal

It was not the first time that Kemp had acted bravely at a fire. When he worked in Birmingham he received press acclaim following a rescue he had undertaken from an upper room of a burning house. Once again, there were suspicions in certain quarters that he was not entitled to the recognition.

Kemp had his sights set on greater things and made at least two unsuccessful applications for chief constable posts at Kidderminster and Leicester. Each one was supported by the chief constable, Carmichael.

In the late summer of 1892, Stephen Winwood, a gardener, told his employer that he had seen Kemp out walking in Pershore meadows in the company of a Mrs Champken. Her husband worked as a baker in a general store in the town, and at the time was training Kemp's son, Victor, in the bakery trade.

Winwood's employer was Pershore miller and Worcester City justice of the peace, George Goodwin. Shocked by what he had heard, he made a point of informing the chief constable, who opened an enquiry into the matter. During the course of his investigation, Carmichael was told by members of the Pershore Bench that Kemp's relationship with Mrs Champken was common knowledge in the town and the magistrates no longer had any confidence in him. The chief constable concluded, after an interview with Kemp, that the superintendent had lied to him and his behaviour amounted to misconduct. He dismissed Kemp in November 1892, shortly before he was due to retire, and, as a consequence, Kemp lost his pension.

At the SJC meeting the following month, Kemp submitted a petition, which was read over to the committee members. The correspondence repeated assertions, made by Kemp to the chief constable, that he was innocent of the allegations, and pleading for his dismissal to be reconsidered. He made a request for the grant of his pension and supported his application with a petition of signatures from residents of Pershore and the surrounding villages. It was all to no avail; his applications were refused. The Archdeacon of Worcester, who was at the meeting, urged the committee to, at the very least, allow a pension to Mrs Kemp, but that was refused as well.

Over the next twelve months or so, Kemp kept up the pressure on the police authority with more letters and petitions asking to be reinstated and allowed his pension, but he was unsuccessful.

Kemp then took action for slander against both Stephen Winwood and George Goodwin, with a view to obtaining damages of £2,000. The hearing was set down for 16th March 1894, at Birmingham Assizes, and the press was there in force. Contemporary newspaper reports indicate that the proceedings were not focussed solely on the incident that gave rise to the action, but on some of Kemp's other activities. A policeman and an ex-policeman were called to blacken the plaintiff's character. If the newspaper accounts were anything to go by, this case gave these men the opportunity to express long-suppressed grievances for past occurrences, dealing with little more than tittle tattle. The evidence exposed the police force to a public examination of a most disagreeable kind. Meanwhile, Counsel for Kemp, Mr A. R. Jelf QC, attacked the chief constable for failing to interview Mr and Mrs Champken during the enquiry which led to Kemp's dismissal.

When all the evidence had been heard, the jury retired for only twenty minutes before returning to find in favour of Henry Kemp and to make an award of £500 damages. The jury was of the view, in the light of their finding, that Kemp should now receive his pension, and had set the figure for damages with that expectation in mind.

The press coverage and support from the police magazine, *Police Review and Parade Gossip,* ensured Kemp received support from far and wide, whilst Mr Goodwin, Mr Winwood and particularly the chief constable were given an extremely difficult time. This pressure increased when it was disclosed that Goodwin had declared himself bankrupt and unable to pay the damages and costs of the proceedings. At the same time (April 1894), Carmichael found himself drawn into correspondence with the *Birmingham Gazette* , but nothing eased the extremely uncomfortable atmosphere.

In the meantime the police authority was at a complete loss to know what to do. At a meeting on Saturday 14th March 1894, two days before the hearing had commenced, it had already pinned its colours to the mast. After much wrangling and deliberation, the thirty-one members present put together two resolutions. In the first, the authority expressed its confidence in the chief constable. The second made it clear that the circumstances surrounding Kemp's dismissal could not be reviewed. This decision was based upon legal advice given to the authority, in accordance with the Police Act of 1890.

By this time the press were baying for blood and calling for action to be taken against the SJC, and particularly against Carmichael, even though the chairman of the SJC, Mr J.W. Willis Bund, had insisted that the decision to sack Kemp was his.

It was not all hostility towards the chief constable, however. Within the force there were letters of support from both serving and former members of the constabulary. Some of the comments, if viewed in current parlance, were completely over the top. An example being "…you are beloved and respected by the whole of your humble servants." Across the county, divisional lists were drawn up, to which policemen added their names in support of the chief constable. Included on the Bromsgrove divisional list was a signature from PC Albert Wargent of Feckenham. He had been stationed at Elmley Castle for part of the time that Superintendent Kemp had been in charge at Pershore. He was also the serving police officer who gave evidence against his former superintendent in the civil proceedings.

A month after the hearing had concluded, Mr Kemp wrote to the chief constable, enclosing a transcript of the judge's summing up and the jury's verdict. Again he asked for reinstatement and his pension or the refund of his pension contributions. Carmichael drew the letter and the transcripts to the attention of the SJC, who were once again advised that legally they could not change the situation.

On 16th July 1894, Mr Schwann, Member of Parliament for Manchester North, asked the Home Secretary, Mr Herbert Asquith MP, if he would allow an independent investigation into the dismissal of Henry Kemp. Schwann was President of the Police and Citizens Association, a group set up to look after the interests of policemen. The Home Secretary refused an investigation but said, "I have caused inquiry to be made, and it is reported to me that the dismissal of Kemp was for untruthfulness more than once repeated; and that the order of dismissal was given by the Chairman of the Worcestershire Standing Joint Committee. The conduct of the chairman is reported to have been approved by a unanimous vote of the Standing Joint Committee."

Twelve months to the day that the matter was raised in the House of Commons, Henry Kemp died at the age of fifty-four. His death raised even more questions about the whole affair. A policeman discovered Kemp's body at about 5.30a.m. in a field at Bricklehampton, a village some three or four miles outside Pershore. The body was lying under a hedge, stiff and cold and away from any footpath. The doctor who examined Kemp said he had died of a heart attack after some exertion, and described the deceased as having some scratches and abrasions on him. Amongst other items, a box, half full with matches, a tobacco pouch and a cigar end were found in Kemp's clothing.

The policeman who found the body was attending a fire at Bricklehampton Hall Farm. The fire had started at about 12.30a.m. and had destroyed several ricks, a dutch barn and two wagons. The seat of the fire was about two hundred yards from the spot where Kemp was found. The owner of the farm, Robert Hinshaw, was a member of the SJC responsible for turning down Kemp's requests. Rumours abounded that Kemp was responsible for the fire. However, those in authority, including HM Coroner, took steps to distance him from the cause of the fire in the absence of conclusive evidence.

There are so many questions left unanswered in this sad affair. Most of them went to the grave with Kemp, leaving the reader to draw his or her own conclusions. At that time there were few checks and balances in place to help a policeman who had been unfairly dealt with, but, did Kemp deserve the treatment he received?

Perhaps he was not all that he seemed. Less than a year before the alleged incident in Pershore meadows, Kemp had a pay cut for four months and was reduced in rank to a lower grade superintendent. The force discipline book shows an entry which reads, "Gross neglect of duty in not having his divisional books made up from 28th August 1891 to 7th October 1891. Giving false certificates every week during that time, that the charges in his division had been entered and indexed. Being untruthful in his replies to the chief constable."

Kemp had a market gardening business operating in Pershore, and on occasions he employed his policemen in horticultural work when they should have been carrying out police duties. For example, Kemp reported to the chief constable that the shaft on the police cart had broken as he stood on it to climb into the driving seat. It subsequently transpired that the shaft had broken whilst Kemp's groom, PC Alfred Sandells, was carrying a load of hay in connection with the superintendent's business. Kemp instructed Sandells to tell lies to the chief constable if questioned about the damage. It has been mentioned elsewhere that the police force sometimes takes a liberal view of many misdemeanours committed by its officers, but rarely treats lying in the same way.

Kemp attributed his errors and inadequacies to his failing mental and physical health combined with an increased workload, and he produced doctors notes in support of his claims. For his part, Carmichael appears to have given Kemp considerable latitude in view of his impending retirement. The Champken incident brought matters to a head and he was obliged to act. Throughout the civil proceedings against Goodwin and Winwood, the chief constable was privately convinced that perjured evidence was being given on behalf of Kemp. It seems reasonable to assume that Superintendent Kemp was extremely lucky to keep his job after the first episode. The second incidence of lying to the chief constable was bound to have terminal consequences.

A former policeman – bad through and through

Kemp was not the only black sheep of the 1890s. Police Constable Charles Young joined the force in 1862. He was a twenty-two-year-old groom from Finstock in Oxfordshire. He spent much of his service in the Pershore division and was eventually promoted to sergeant in 1870 and posted to Broadway. By 1874 he had moved to Wychbold, from where he was dismissed for unspecified immoral conduct.

Young travelled to the U.S.A. and it was alleged that he was arrested there on more than twenty occasions. Each time, it seems he was able to avoid a conviction.

Young obtained ownership of a saloon, which was eventually mortgaged up to the hilt. He tried to sell it to an acquaintance, and accepted a deposit from him without revealing the financial burdens. When the prospective purchaser discovered that he had been duped, he refused to pay the balance of the monies due. In response the former policeman drew a revolver and shot the man and his wife at point blank range. Fortunately their injuries, although serious, were not fatal.

Charles Young was soon arrested, and when he appeared before a court he was granted bail to await his trial. He promptly fled the country, returning to England but, after extradition proceedings, he was returned to America to stand trial on a charge of "shooting with intent to kill". At the conclusion of the hearing Young was found guilty of "intent to do grievous bodily harm" and he was sentenced to four years, imprisonment. He appealed against the conviction and, once more, luck was on his side. It transpired that he could only be convicted of the offence for which he had been extradited, and so his conviction was overturned. Young returned to England and, in December 1894, commenced what proved to be a futile application to the American Government for compensation.

The story then moves to Lowesmoor, Worcester, where, on Thursday 14th January 1895, Detective Inspector Thomas Wallace, of the City Police, was keeping two men under observation. One of the men answered the description of a man who was suspected of stealing a pony and trap at Doncaster. The suspect man was trying to sell a pony and trap to the other man, named Hughes.

Wallace approached the suspect, and was able to persuade him to accompany him to the city police station. There he was seen by the city chief constable, Mr Byrne. The suspect gave his name as Frank Evans. He agreed that he had been trying to sell a pony and trap that he kept at his home in Drakes Broughton. He told the policemen that he was a farmer and market gardener with a small holding of eight acres. He offered a number of names of well known Pershore people who he claimed could vouch for him, and Mr Byrne suggested that the police should wire one of them for confirmation. Evans offered to go with Wallace to Drakes Broughton to sort things out and to pay any costs incurred. Although Evans fitted the bill for the Doncaster offence, he was so plausible during the interview that, not only were the policemen taken in, they didn't search him because he was not under arrest.

Wallace and Evans set off in a cab, which eventually dropped them off at the Pinvin crossroads, from where Evans described the subsequent journey as "…about a quarter of an hour's sharp walk". Both men walked towards Pershore railway station, then left the main road to take a back lane towards Drakes Broughton. When they got to an isolated spot, Wallace walked ahead of Evans, who produced a revolver and shot him in the back. He continued to fire until the gun was empty. Wallace was struck by at least four of the six bullets, but picked up a stick and beat Evans until he fell backwards into a nearby brook. Wallace by now was feeling the effects of losing a lot of blood and could not pursue Evans, who climbed out of the water on the opposite bank and ran off.

Detective Inspector Wallace's shouts for help alerted a number of people, who came to help him. Some of them followed Evans' footprints in the snow for some distance before eventually catching up with him on the outskirts of Worcester. They kept the man under observation until he got to Edgar Street near the city centre. There they sought the assistance of Sergeant Harley, of the city police, who was able to take Evans into custody.

When Evans was later interviewed by Colonel Carmichael, he admitted that he was former policeman Charles Young. He was charged with attempting to murder Thomas Wallace. When he appeared before Worcester County Assizes he pleaded not guilty, but was convicted by the jury. As the judge imposed a sentence of twenty years penal servitude, his decision was applauded by members of the public seated in the court.

Detective Inspector Wallace spent some time recovering from his injuries before returning to duty. He was an extremely popular man, both within and outside the police service. As a result of the incident he was awarded £30 by the Watch Committee. A further collection within the community produced more than £70, which he received at a special presentation later the same year.

Unacceptable behaviour

The following examples give an insight into the life of the Victorian policeman. Whilst some are amusing, others would be treated seriously no matter when they occurred.

In 1880, PC Charles Littlefield was the constable at Cutnall Green. He was severely reprimanded and moved to Redditch, at his own expense, for failing to keep conference points. He also refused to get out of bed to attend a fire in the early hours of one morning, telling his wife to say that he was already out. He didn't improve his ways at Redditch and he was sacked ten days later, only four months after he had joined.

PC Henry Hooper was admonished and cautioned when "…he raffled his watch at a private house in Pershore on 27th October 1883, having sold between thirty and forty tickets at 1/- (5p) each."

PC Joseph Mason, a married man, was ordered to resign on 30th April 1880, when it was discovered that he "…had sexual intercourse with a girl named Ellen Hawkes on two occasions on a Sunday afternoon, at Hanley Castle, in full uniform and in broad daylight. His behaviour being witnessed by two men and some children."

PC John Bateman "…absconded from his duty all night having spent the time in one of the dens of Dudley with some of the lowest characters." Bateman was arrested on warrant, taken before the Dudley magistrates and fined 10/- (50p) with costs. He was dismissed on 30th June 1880.

PC George Jones "…left Malvern police station all night on 20th February 1882, attending a Ball at the Drill Hall without permission. When ordered to return at

2.45a.m. by Sergeant Drury, refused to do so." Jones was reduced from 2nd class to 3rd class constable and fined two days' pay – 6/- (30p).

PC Henry Bedford was fined £2.0.0d by a magistrates and dismissed by the chief constable on 24th July 1882 for "...stealing a sovereign out of a cupboard in the dwelling house of PC John Harvey at Dudley." Bedford had already been in trouble earlier in the same year. He "...was severely reprimanded for his carelessness when at Dudley he negligently omitted to lock a cell door, thereby allowing a prisoner to escape."

It is an ill wind that blows nobody any good as, on the same date, PC William Sherriff was commended by the Chief Constable for "promptitude and success in recapturing a prisoner for felony, who had escaped from the Dudley police cells."

PC Edward Griffiths, stationed at Dudley, was required to resign on 14th January 1883, when he was "...absent from his beat for more than two hours while on night duty and having no qualification for a constable, being stupid and useless."

In 1886, PC James Agg fell foul of an anonymous-letter writer who informed the chief constable that Agg was selling refreshments, from his police station at Arley, to tourists visiting the area. He escaped with a caution. When he did again in 1889 he was fined three days' pay.

PC James Agg
Stourbridge 1903

PC Michael Waldron was dismissed on 30th April 1886, because "...he was dilatory generally. For contracting debts he could not or would not pay. Disobedience of orders. Absent from his beat. Drunk while on duty and assaulting the Vicar of Studley, at Redditch, by striking him on the head as he passed along the street on the night of 27th April 1886."

PC Samuel Davis was reprimanded and cautioned for "...neglect of duty at Stourbridge by not turning down the gas lights thereby causing waste and sleeping on duty." PC Davis again, "...was severely reprimanded for boxing with gloves on, at a public house at Kinver (Staffs) in plain clothes, after giving evidence there before the magistrates on behalf of two men who had been summoned for drunkenness."

On 31st December 1887, PC Thomas Clarke was cautioned "...not to do so again and to express his regret for forgetting himself, to Mr Burton (Chief Superintendent Henry Burton at Dudley), following his disobedience of orders by wearing a vest in a slovenly manner under his uniform after being cautioned by the chief superintendent."

In August 1888, PC Thomas Gall, who was stationed at Bretforton, was found "...to be spending a considerable portion of his time in haymaking having purchased nine acres of mowing grass for Mr E Kings for whom he engaged a number of men and women to make hay." He was reprimanded, cautioned and directed to hold himself in readiness for removal to some other station. He was posted to Ripple in October 1888. (When the haymaking was over?)

On 12th June 1889, PC George Ellison was fined three days' pay, 10/6d (52½p), and severely reprimanded "...when at Hartlebury after leaving his beat without permission, getting drunk at Astley and being asleep all night in a field."

**PC George Ellison
Malvern 1899**

Nurse Elizabeth

Before the force had sufficient time to recover from the Kemp fiasco, it was plunged into a situation that was not of its own making, but which drew much public attention because it involved a policeman.

Robert Narramore joined the Worcestershire Constabulary in 1884. He was a married man with two daughters. In 1890 he was posted to Clent as the local sergeant. When his wife became ill he sought the services of Nurse Elizabeth Brandish to look after her. Nurse Elizabeth, as she was commonly known, attended Jane Narramore until she died in December 1896. During the time Elizabeth was with the Narramore family, the daughters, Emily and Charlotte, became very attached to her, whilst she formed a close relationship with Sergeant Narramore. There was no suggestion of anything improper, but it seems that both Narramore and the nurse had it in mind to get married when a respectable time had elapsed after Jane's death.

What Narramore and his family did not know was that Nurse Elizabeth had a secret. She was born in about 1864 and was a native of Little Compton in Warwickshire. Her father and grandfather had been the landlords of the Red Lion, the only pub in the village. She had worked as a barmaid and does not appear to have travelled far from her home until she is alleged to have had an affair with a married man, which left her pregnant. The liaison did not continue and she gave birth to a little boy in Kent. She made arrangements for the boy, named Rees Thomas Yells Brandish, to be looked after by an elderly couple near Ashford. She paid 5/- (25p) a week for his keep. The arrangement lasted for about two and a half years, during which time she struck up her acquaintance with the Narramore family.

In September 1897 Elizabeth went to collect her son from Kent, telling the family that she was intending to go into business and wanted the boy with her. This proved to be untrue. The family had grown quite attached to the little boy, and their suspicions were aroused when the mother insisted that she took the child, with just the clothes he stood up in.

Superintendent Alfred Pugh c1904

Elizabeth made a number of train journeys with the little boy, but by the time she returned to her brother's home near Ettington, Rees had disappeared.

Eventually, Elizabeth returned to Clent where she was seen by Superintendent Alfred Pugh. He had received a letter from Kent that expressed concerns about the boy's wellbeing. Pugh explained why he was there and Elizabeth immediately explained that she had a child and had given him to a lady who wanted a child. Unfortunately, she was unable to say who the lady was.

Meanwhile, the Warwickshire police went to Elizabeth's brother's home and dug up the body of a child. It had been buried in the garden and covered in quicklime. Forensic science being in its early stages meant that an examination of the body revealed very little of use. It proved to be impossible to identify the child, although it was estimated to be a well nourished two and a half year old.

The Warwickshire police felt they had enough evidence and arrested Nurse Elizabeth at Clent. She was tried at Warwickshire Assizes in March 1898 for the murder of her son. She denied the offence and the jury was unable to agree.

In July 1898 she again stood trial, and even faced the introduction of new evidence concerning letters she had written that tended to prove her knowledge of the offence. Newspaper interest was intense and Robert Narramore had to give evidence concerning their relationship at each trial. When the second jury returned to the courtroom to give its verdict, the Judge had his black cap with him as if the case was a forgone conclusion. However, the jury did not agree and Nurse Elizabeth was discharged.

Murder of a gamekeeper

In November 1889 and subsequent weeks the murder of a gamekeeper and the arrest of his assailants held the headlines of county newspapers.

Frederick Stephens was employed as a gamekeeper by the Duc d'Aumale on his estate on the outskirts of Evesham. As Stephens made his way home at about 2.00a.m. on Sunday 10th November he saw three men, with dogs, walking in the woods. It was a moonlit night and he saw that each man had a bag. Stephens approached the men and, as he got close to them, one man, Joseph Boswell, said, "Let him have it."

Each of the men began to throw stones at the gamekeeper. None of them hit him, but one of the men struck him with his fist and knocked him to the ground. Another of the men tried to throttle him as he lay on the ground. In doing so the man placed a finger in the gamekeeper's mouth, and got it severely bitten. Stephens was then kicked about the head and body by each of the men, one of whom beat him across the back. When the men left, Stephens lost consciousness for several minutes. When he came to, he staggered for about a mile to the house of the head keeper, Benjamin Wasley. Wasley took the injured man by horse and trap into Evesham, to report what had happened to the police and to be treated by Doctor Haynes.

Stephens was confined to his sickbed and made two depositions to Mr Cox, Clerk to the Evesham justices. On both occasions he identified Joseph Boswell as one of his attackers. He died some days later from the head injuries inflicted by his attackers.

Within a few days, three brothers named Boswell had been arrested by the police, but in due course it became apparent that one of the brothers, James, was not involved. This left Joseph and Samuel Boswell in custody. The search was then on for the third man, who had been identified as Alfred Hill. Hill had moved to Birmingham where he was working under an assumed name. He was traced by the Birmingham police to Windsor Street gas works. To ensure that they got the right man, a young policeman named PC Charles Bayliss, who came from Evesham and knew Hill, was chosen to go into the gas works to find him. Bayliss, dressed as a gas worker and with his face blacked, was able to get close to Hill and arrest him, but not without a violent struggle.

The three defendants came up for trial at the Worcester Assizes in February 1890. At the end of the first day's hearing, the jurors were conveyed to the Unicorn Hotel in a large wagonette and were accommodated in the inappropriately named 'Glee Room'. The next day, the jury was treated to an early morning drive in the country by way of Crown East. They were allowed to purchase their morning newspapers before settling back in their seats in the courtroom. Pressure for seats elsewhere in the court was considerable, as many members of the public crowded in to hear the proceedings. The deputy chief constable, Alfred Tyler, earned the praise of the *Berrows Worcester Journal* for his efforts in keeping the corridors and passages clear whilst allowing maximum seating. The day's proceedings lasted from 10.30a.m. until 9.30p.m. when the jury retired to consider the evidence whilst Judge Hawkins dined.

Shortly before midnight the jury returned. It soon became apparent that their agreement on the guilt of the men was complete, except for one juryman. The judge proceeded to lecture the jury on the duties of each of its members, and as he did so he gesticulated with the ivory handled toothpick he had been using a little earlier to pick his teeth. As he concluded his rebuke he threatened to isolate the jury for a further twelve hours to enable a unanimous verdict. Throughout the judge's speech, members of the jury focussed their collective attention upon a member sitting in the second row. This left little doubt as to the identity of the dissenter. The combined pressures of the scolding from the judge, the irritation of his colleagues and, no doubt, the embarrassed isolation he must have felt, encouraged the lone juror to reconsider his position and join the majority. The verdict of guilty opened the way for Judge Hawkins to sentence the men to death by hanging, which he duly did.

The date for the execution was set as 11th March 1890. The gallows had last been used for the execution of Moses Shrimpton, who had been convicted of the murder of PC James Davis in 1885. The *Berrows Worcester Journal* recorded the fact that the gallows had to be extended to enable the three men to stand side by side in their final moments.

Almost immediately after the murderers were sentenced, a petition was drawn up to request their reprieve. Within a very short time, 2,500 signatures were gathered, many of them from Worcester citizens. A number of prominent residents were moved to write directly to the Home Secretary, expressing similar views.

The vicar of Evesham, Reverend B Straffen, used the case as the subject of a sermon in which he drew comparisons with David's killing of Goliath. As he warmed to his subject he began to expound his views on cursing, bad language, rioting and drunkenness. Meanwhile there was much concern expressed for the young families of the condemned men, and supporters raised funds to help the wives and children.

The day before the executions were due to take place, the Home Secretary notified the county authorities of his decision to reprieve Hill. This was a decision that most observers found difficult to understand, particularly as there was a view in some quarters that he had behaved worst of the three in the attack.

The following morning, at about 7.30a.m., a crowd of about fifty people gathered outside the county gaol as city policemen took up positions to control them. By the time the flag was raised over the building, signifying the completion of the executions, the crowd had swelled to more than a thousand. Members of the press were permitted to witness the proceedings as the executioner, Mr Berry, prepared the scaffold and secured the prisoners. When he pulled the bolt on the trapdoor he brought a most controversial case to a close..

Chapter Six

A statutory pension

The introduction of the Police Act of 1890 brought new security to the Victorian policeman and his family. For the first time he was given the assurance of a pension after twenty-five years' service, with a medical pension available after fifteen. There were also benefits for police families who lost their breadwinner whilst he was on duty. The legislation included an optional proviso that allowed police authorities to set a minimum starting age before contributions towards a pension became effective. Worcestershire was one of the few forces to utilise this clause. As a result, recruits below the age of twenty-one were required to sign a document to acknowledge that their contributions would not take effect until they were twenty-one.

The new legislation also meant that the finances of the superannuation fund would now remain stable. Throughout its history, the fund had been troubled by inadequate resourcing. By the end of 1880 it was reported to be £317 overdrawn. The county had been borrowing from the account for years to finance building projects, including a number of schools, police stations and Holt Fleet bridge. The loans did continue because the interest raised by them was far too lucrative to ignore, but they were not allowed to drain the fund.

New boundaries – new buildings

In 1889 the Borough of Birmingham gained city status and almost immediately sought to incorporate adjacent parts of Worcestershire within its boundaries. The first to succumb (but not the last) was Balsall Heath. On 9th November 1891 some of the officers serving there, PC Peter Clarke, PC William Squires, PC John Taylor, PC Thomas Rees Williams, PC Richard Aston, PC Thomas Harris and PC Francis Osborne transferred to the Birmingham City Police. The agreement included the sale of Edward Road police station for £5,250.

On 1st October 1899 the Parish of Yardley was transferred from Warwickshire to Worcestershire. It was the return of a part of Worcestershire that had been annexed in August 1857. With the transfer came seven policemen, two police stations, namely Acocks Green and Sparkhill, as well as fourteen police houses at Sparkhill, Hay Mills, Acocks Green, Greet, Stechford, Yardley and Yardley Wood.

From Fruit Trees to Furnaces - A History of the Worcestershire Constabulary   59

PC Peter Clarke
c1887

The district of Yardley was added to an already large Northfield Division, under the command of Superintendent James Wasley. To enable him to supervise the area adequately, he was provided with a second horse, extra expenses and an increase in wages of 1/6d (7½p) a day.

In 1893 the SJC agreed that the Pershore divisional headquarters should move to Evesham. To obtain additional space, a burned-out house next door to the Oat Street police station was purchased for £175. When the house was demolished and the site cleared, a police house and an extension to the weights and measures office were built on the land.

A similar decision was made in the Upton division in 1897 when the divisional headquarters at Upton were moved to Malvern, reflecting the rapid increase occurring in the population there.

In 1895, plans for the construction of a new police station at Redditch led to the selection of a plot of land, owned by Lord Windsor, fronting onto Evesham Street, Ludlow Road and Oakly Road. Several months elapsed before a decision was made to shelve the idea for twelve months. In May 1896 Thomas Field approached the SJC, offering land in Church Road for £1,000. Here there was sufficient room to build a police station and a court room, with surplus land available if required. The offer was accepted.

The contract to build the new complex was awarded to C. G. Huins and Sons of Alcester Street, Redditch, but progress was not good. Building did not start until 1898 and the work was plagued by shortages of bricks, bricklayers, stonemasons and, finally, plasterers. The SJC became extremely agitated and made the life of the county surveyor, Henry Rowe, who was supervising the work, something of a misery. After a number of promised completion dates passed without the occupation of the premises, it was a very relieved Rowe who reported with confidence that the buildings would be ready for occupation soon after 6th May 1899. It was just as well that he was right, because the SJC immediately agreed to sell the old police station to Redditch Urban District Council for £1,350.

A shortage of skilled labour also held up the building of Halesowen police station in 1899. The contractor, J H Whittaker of Dudley, had difficulties getting bricklayers and, towards the end of the contract, carpenters, who had been on strike. The premises were eventually occupied in May 1900.

At Stirchley the county purchased a piece of land on the corner of Mary Vale Road and Victoria Road to build a new police station. Fortunately for Mr Rowe, the building work, which started towards the end of 1898, went extremely smoothly and the premises were ready for occupation in November the following year. The builder on this occasion was Samuel Cheese from Worcester. In spite of the distance from his base, Cheese was able to provide the cheapest tender, £3,050, out of the eleven submitted.

The police station at Acocks Green was a small house in a terrace that had been built in 1879. It provided living accommodation for a sergeant and his family, a charge room and four cells (unusually, two on the ground floor and two directly above them). The cells were each fitted with a WC and were approached by a dark, confined passage and a narrow stairway. It was decided that the premises were no longer suitable for police purposes and, as there was no room to extend, they were earmarked for replacement. The shortage of space at the police station meant that the local magistrates court was held in the public hall a few hundred yards away. The public hall committee charged 10/- (50p) for every day the court sat. At one stage the public hall committee offered to sell the hall to the police authority for £3,000, but the cost of converting the premises proved to be prohibitive and the proposition was declined.

The growth of the force and the requirements of its administration meant that space at the headquarters in Loves Grove had become totally inadequate. The premises doubled as the head police office for the county and all that went with it, as well as the divisional headquarters for the county portion of the area which immediately surrounded Worcester. More and more room was needed for stores and equipment, and to provide for greater numbers of recruits.

The main office was utilised as the charge room. Prisoners were placed in one of three cells, which had no proper sanitation and required soil buckets. Single men were accommodated in a large bedroom on the first floor and slept on mattresses that were at least as hard as the bedsteads that supported them. The floor of the bedroom was constructed from rough floorboards, each one possessing splinters that lay in wait to pierce an unsuspecting bare foot. The housekeeper was a Mrs Hughes, who had been widowed some years before. She was described as a homely sort who looked after the young men as if they were members of her own family.

In 1898 the chief constable told the police authority that the building was at bursting point. Fortunately he had identified a suitable site in Castle Street, a short distance away, which would fit the bill. The property was being offered for sale by the Trustees of the Worcester Infirmary. There was enough room to provide sufficient accommodation for all foreseen police requirements. Additionally, space was available to build private quarters for the deputy chief constable and the chief clerk, as well as the drill sergeant/storekeeper, and their families. When plans were drawn up, they included rooms for ten single men, a men's room, a sick room, an ablutions room and a recreation room.

**Former Worcestershire Police Headquarters, Castle Street, Worcester c1965.
The Chief Constable's office was on the first floor over the open doorway.**

Although the county had quite a forward-looking building programme underway, there were some police premises that left a lot to be desired. Ombersley station was a prime example. It comprised a house and two cells, which were on a lease at £7.10.0d (£7.50) per annum from Lord Sandys.

The chief constable described the premises in a report to the SJC in 1899. "There are two cells which are approached through...the kitchen, and are in such close proximity to the dwelling rooms that every blasphemous word and coarse expression used by the prisoners is within hearing of the family of the police officer." The house was situated at the crossroads in Ombersley. Complaints of cramped and insanitary conditions led to a notice being served, in 1898, upon the police authority by the sanitary inspector of Droitwich Rural District Council, in respect of the drainage. The kitchen, which measured 13' 4" by 13', had three doors, one of which led to the cell area. Upstairs there were two bedrooms. At the time of Carmichael's report, Sergeant William Hanley lived at the station with his wife Edith and their seven children.

Sergeant William Hanley
Loves Grove, Worcester
June, 1903

To ease the problem the Sandys Estate offered the county an adjoining property, known as Filmer House, on a twenty-one-year lease at £19 per annum. The offer was accepted and it was agreed that cells would be built and alterations made, up to a maximum cost of £230. The new police station was occupied shortly before Christmas 1899.

Whilst the police authority struggled with the requirements of a growing police force, the members of the constabulary continued to deal with the events that life presented them with.

A nasty murder

On 19th July 1893, Arnie Holman Meunier, a twenty-five-year-old Frenchman, was executed at Worcester gaol for the brutal murder of Charlotte Pearcey, at Bromsgrove. In January 1893, Meunier was peddling cheap stationary and pencils at Lickey End, claiming to represent a charity for the deaf and dumb. It was in this guise that he visited Mrs Pearcey's shop in Little Heath Lane. A few days later, he paid a further visit to the shop and this time he battered Mrs Pearcey to death. As he ransacked the rooms, he was seen by Mr Pearcey, who was ill in bed. Realising that he could now be identified, Meunier fled to Belgium, but was quickly traced by police and brought back to Worcestershire to face trial. The hearing was at the Assizes, before Baron Polluck. Meunier was convicted and sentenced to death.

Merit badges and rewards

Drinking and driving is not a modern phenomenon; in fact, it pre-dates the invention of the motor car. In 1893, Joseph Alcock, an Evesham chemist, was seen to be helplessly rolling around in the back of his cart, as his horse meandered from one side of Vine Street to the other. PC Ernest Gittus was on duty in plain clothes and stepped out to stop the horse. The chemist begged the officer not to report the matter, but PC Gittus was not inclined to do so and soon, Alcock was able to tell the magistrates his tale of woe.

Ernest Gittus, a native of Himbleton, was one of three brothers who served in the county force. He joined in 1889 and Evesham was his first posting. In 1894 he was awarded a merit badge and £2 reward for meritorious conduct, when he rescued a woman from the River Avon after being called from his bed in the early hours one morning. This was a particularly brave act because, apart from the time of the year, when the water must have been freezing cold, the undercurrents of the river near to the town centre have a tendency to draw bodies to the bottom.

PC Ernest Gittus
Malvern 1899

There are numerous examples of policemen displaying great courage to effect a rescue or to avoid injury to members of the public. Success meant that the policeman was usually financially rewarded and received a merit badge, but failure could result in serious injury and no job. The merit badge was a crescent-shaped piece of cloth embroidered in white cotton with the word 'Merit'. The recipient was permitted to wear it on the right sleeve of his tunic, above the elbow.

In 1898, PC Edward Hadley was rewarded for a rescue at Stourport. Whilst patrolling in Engine Lane, wearing his full uniform, including a greatcoat, PC Hadley saw a group of boys playing at the canal basin. As the officer approached the group, one of them, Luke Knott, fell in. The boy began to struggle. He sank in about ten feet of water. Hadley was not a swimmer but he jumped into the water fully clothed and succeeded in bringing the boy to the side of the basin safely. He received a merit badge and a reward.

PC Edward Hadley
Stourport c1898

In 1899, just two days after Christmas, PC George Clinton was involved in another watery rescue when he was on duty in Cannon Hill Park. There were a large number of people skating on an ice-covered pool and, as he watched, the ice broke and five children fell into the freezing water. The officer went to their rescue, but found that the ice broke under his weight, so he jumped into the water, which came up to his shoulders. He was able to save each of the children, but was unable to get out of the water because the ice continued to break around him as he tried to scramble out. Fortunately someone was able to bring a ladder, and with the aid of onlookers he was able to get to dry land. PC Clinton received a merit badge and a reward of £2. In 1900 he received the Royal Humane Society's certificate for the rescue.

PC George Clinton
Halesowen 1910

At an SJC meeting on 6th May 1899, the bravery of PC John Hemming was recognised when he was awarded a merit badge and a reward of £2. Hemming was on duty in Church Street, Bromsgrove, on 16th April when a young cart horse, harnessed to a cartload of bricks, took fright in Churchfields and galloped away with a twelve-year-old boy on board. One of the men assisting in unloading the cart tried to stop the horse, but fell under it and was trampled to death. The officer saw the approach of the careering horse and cart and "…with great pluck and skill and at considerable personal risk…" was able to stop the frightened animal.

On Thursday 12th July 1900, a pair of heavy cart horses, harnessed to a dray, were standing near the Lamb and Flag Inn at Unicorn Hill in Redditch. As the dray was being unloaded the animals became frightened by a sudden clap of thunder, and ran away at great speed down Unicorn Hill. PC Harry Owen was on duty near the spot. In considerable danger, he managed to catch the reins and, after being dragged some distance, successfully stop the horses.

Harry Owen received a merit badge and a reward of £2. He was forty-three when this incident took place, having been a policeman for more than twenty-three years. He must have had some very strong personal qualities, because he had been disciplined on no fewer than six occasions, including an appearance before Chipping Campden magistrates, when he was convicted for an offence of assault and fined £1 with 15/- (75p) costs. An officer with a disciplinary record such as this would not normally expect his services to be retained for very long. However, he went on to complete more than twenty-six years service and was granted a pension in 1903.

At 12.50a.m. on 23rd July 1900, PC James Dumbleton, stationed at Sparkhill, was on night duty in Fraser Road, Greet, when he detected a strong smell of gas coming from the home of Henry Rudge. The officer quickly removed his lamp from his belt, tied a handkerchief over his mouth and went into the house, which was full of gas. He then discovered Mrs Louisa Rudge, who had been overcome by the gas, and he carried her outside. He applied artificial respiration until she regained consciousness. Dumbleton again entered the house and was able to stop the escape of gas, which had been caused by a tap left full on. He opened the doors and windows, then went upstairs where he found Mr Rudge lying on the bed, fully dressed and semi-conscious. The officer took him outside where he soon recovered. PC Dumbleton was rewarded with £2 and a merit badge. He later received the Royal Humane Society's certificate and bronze medal, which was presented to him by the Lord Mayor of Birmingham on 11th December 1900.

Early in 1902, Sergeant William Cooper and PC William Fitzer averted what could have been a disaster at the Noah's Ark public house at Stourbridge. The landlord, Mr Welch, went to the cellar to skim beer that was fermenting. The room was filled with strong carbonic acid fumes and he was overcome. A similar fate was suffered by his wife when she went to help him. Four men who were in the public house went to the cellar to assist and each of them lost consciousness. The landlord's daughter called upon Sergeant Cooper to help, and with the aid of his colleague he was able to vent the cellar and carry the casualties to safety. Both men received awards from the Royal Humane Society and the Standing Joint Committee.

Sergeant William Cooper and PC William Fitzer c1902

Fred Gegg was an Evesham photographer who, amongst other photographic works, did a brisk trade in photographing policemen in uniform, as individuals or in large groups. On 6th February 1902, his house went up in flames, due no doubt to the chemicals he stored there. PC Edward Poulson attended the fire and smashed a window to gain access. In doing so he suffered a nasty gash on his wrist, which rendered him unfit for duty for five days. He received a merit badge and a £2 reward. The records do not show whether PC Poulson was trying to deal with the fire, or attempting to rescue a recently taken photograph of himself.

Injuries to policemen

Many police officers become victims, simply because of who they are. They are often attacked because they try to prevent the law being broken or, where there is a breach, they are set upon when they attempt to make an arrest. Nothing much has changed in this respect over the years.

PC John Hill joined the constabulary in April 1887, at the age of nineteen years. He was a native of St Johns, Worcester. His first posting was to Dudley, but he resigned two years later. Within two months he had rejoined and was posted to Oldswinford near Stourbridge. He married Ellen Mercer, also of St Johns, in 1890. She found it very difficult to adapt to the ways of the police force and was extremely concerned about her husband's safety, so much so that she threatened to leave him if he did not resign, so he did. It took him two months to talk Ellen around and to allow him to rejoin the police force, but Ellen's fears were well founded. Whilst stationed at Inkberrow her husband was badly assaulted at Holberrow Green, suffering an eye injury that kept him off duty for twelve days. Three men were later each sentenced to two months' hard labour for the attack on him. In 1900, he was forced to take sick leave again. The eye that had suffered injury in the attack had become diseased. He was unable to return to work and, after being on the sick list for eight months, had to retire on a pension of £36.10.0d (£36.50) per annum.

Injuries to policemen were becoming a serious problem for the force in the 1890s. Whether caused by violence or by an accident, the loss of policemen from duty caused manpower difficulties. In 1894, PC Frank Short was off duty for two days because he had been kicked whilst arresting a prisoner. PC Alfred Jones was struck on the head with a brick as well as being badly assaulted at Rood End in the Halesowen division. He was unable to return to duty for fourteen days. His assailant, Thomas Hill, was sentenced to twelve months' hard labour. PC Jared Walters, whilst stationed at Malvern, was off duty for fifteen days when he was bitten on the hand whilst arresting Jacob Curtis.

On 6th November 1900, PC Herbert Hartland was on night duty at Yardley when he stopped two men, one of whom was carrying a sack of stolen fowl. There was a violent struggle in which Hartland was bitten, and kicked in the head until he was unconscious. He had succeeded in handcuffing one of the men, but both men were able to escape. One of the offenders, Samuel Scrivener, was later arrested and subsequently sentenced to fifteen months' hard labour. Mr Justice Wright, who heard the case, was particularly impressed by the officer's bravery and expressed his regret that he was unable to reward him. However, he took the matter up with the chief constable, who awarded Hartland a merit badge and £2 reward.

PC Herbert Hartland
Bromsgrove 1905

PC William Banks had a similar experience when he tackled three men who were out poaching on the outskirts of Kidderminster one night in November 1901. He was struck on the head with a half brick and then stoned until he was unconscious. He remained senseless for about three-quarters of an hour. Later he received a £2 reward and a merit badge for his bravery.

In some cases, apparently simple injuries put paid to an officer's career. PC Ishmael Hall had his fair share of suffering when, in October 1896, he received a fractured left ankle-bone whilst ejecting John Craddock from the Victoria Inn at Dudley Wood. He was off duty for more than three months. In October 1899, he was bitten on the same leg by a dog set on him by William Humphreys of Quarry Bank and Ernest Humphreys from Lye, when he attempted to take them into custody for being drunk and disorderly. He was off duty for forty days. The final crunch (if that is the right word) came when he was making a conference point at 1.00a.m. on 2nd December 1900. Ishmael slipped over on some loose cinders, breaking a small bone in his left leg. On this occasion he was off duty for almost a year before retiring on 30th November 1901. Less than two months later he was dead. He had served for twenty-three and a half years.

Records of accidental injuries include PC George Biddle, who fell down one frosty night at Dudley, on a slippery pavement. He broke two bones in his right leg. Problems arising from this injury continued to trouble him for some time and two years later he had to retire on medical grounds. PC Henry Groves, from Bengeworth, Evesham, was off duty for fifteen days when he injured his knee whilst trying to stop a runaway horse and trap. Sergeant Albert Parry was injured at Kings Heath in 1900 when he was thrown from a trap on his way to Moor Green Lane, Kings Heath in search of fowl stealers. He suffered three fractured ribs and was off duty for seventy days. On 21st December 1900, PC Alfred Clark, from Astwood Bank, went to the Woodman Inn after receiving some information that a man wanted by Pershore police could be found there. Whilst making a search of the premises he missed his footing and fell down some steps. As he fell, he hit his head, fracturing his skull. The injury proved fatal.

The death of a serving police officer is always received with a collective heavy heart within the police service. It is a time when the force becomes a large family. The long illness of PC Henry Patten is a sad case in point. Henry Patten became a policeman in 1887 at the age of eighteen, having worked as a gardener at Bockleton near Tenbury. He was a married man with two children and had served at Upton, Wribbenhall and finally Franche, where he was taken ill on 10th July 1898. The police surgeon, Dr Hyde, certified that he was suffering from tuberculosis and said he would never be fit for police duty again. In spite of this prognosis there was no rush to discharge him from the force. He was allowed a leave of absence, during which time he visited Weston super Mare and the Isle of Man, but to no great benefit. On 7th April 1899 he embarked on the steamer 'Tintagel' on a return voyage to the Cape of Good Hope. It was hoped that the holiday would improve his health. He made the journey by himself, the cost of the trip being made up by contributions from his colleagues and a local collection organised by Reverend Parker, the curate of Franche. The steamer proprietors, Messrs Donald Currie and Co., also offered a twenty-per-cent reduction on their normal charges. When he returned from South Africa on 16th June he was described as being very feeble. He died on 10th July 1899. His widow, Jane, received a gratuity of £66.18.4d (£66.92).

A wage review

In the years leading to the end of the nineteenth century, the county police force continued to rapidly increase its numbers. Applications were being submitted regularly to the Home Office, to seek approval for the establishment of additional police cover in areas where it had previously been inadequate or to reflect industrial or population movements. Recruiting was steady, but the chief constable had already drawn the loss of many men to the attention of the police authority. A number of officers, having been trained at the expense of the county, transferred to the better-paid Birmingham City police force. In fact, police wages in Worcestershire did not measure up well against those of most surrounding forces. A review of the pay structure led to a wage increase, which did much to stem the flow of good officers from the force.

Boer war

From 1899 through to 1900 eight policemen were recalled to the colours to fight in the Boer War. They were PCs William Cooke, William Gould, Charles Haden, John Hemming, Samuel Roberts, James Tolley, William Walters and John White. Sadly, two of them did not return. James Tolley was killed in action at Belmont, South Africa. He was unmarried but left his elderly parents, who lived at Hanley Castle. William Walters died of dysentery at Naauwport, South Africa on 16th June 1900. His widowed mother was his sole dependant.

PC William Walters
Stourport 1898

Departure of the deputy chief constable

On 31st March 1900, the deputy chief constable, John Wheeler, announced his intention to retire at the end of June. He had been in the post for eight years. In a report to the SJC he asked to be allowed a pension as he was "…of advancing age and failing health." He was sixty-four years of age and attributed his deteriorating condition, in part, to being "…called upon to perform many difficult and dangerous duties, the carrying out of which has resulted in many instances in very serious assaults being committed upon me by criminals I have had to arrest…". Superintendent James Wasley succeeded Wheeler as DCC.

John Wheeler
Deputy Chief Constable
1892 - 1900

Communications

From 1885 onwards, the gradual introduction of telephones into the force, placed the constabulary at the forefront of communications. Carmichael had quickly appreciated the benefits that telephones could provide. Indeed, by the turn of the century all the main stations had a telephone, including some private lines operating within some stations.

Communications with stations that were not included on the telephone network continued to be fairly primitive. In fact, some events overtook the message, as PC Alfred Pass experienced first hand. In 1899, he was promoted to sergeant and posted to Kings Heath. Unfortunately, the message containing details of his promotion had not got to him. At 9.00 a.m. on Monday 9th October 1899, a horse-drawn removal van arrived at his home in Broadway. It was to take his family, including two young daughters, and all their possessions to Kings Heath. His wife, Jane, was busy washing clothes and Alfred Pass was already out on patrol. The problems that this event created must have been quite traumatic for Jane Pass. Nothing was packed away and there was a tub of wet washing to be dealt with. Her biggest fear was that another family would turn up, wanting to move in before she was ready. Loading the van took a while, and in the meantime PC Pass returned home. The family still had to face a long journey and it was not until it was approaching midnight that they arrived at their new home. There was nothing to do except prepare a quick meal and sleep where they could. Sergeant Pass was on duty the next day.

Some years later, whilst stationed at Selly Oak, Inspector Alfred Pass generated some interest when he summoned himself. One night he was on duty at the station when he set the chimney alight. This was an offence and he dealt with it by issuing a summons to himself. He appeared before the next petty sessions and pleaded guilty. Mr Cadbury, the chairman of the bench, ordered him to pay costs of 7/6d (37½p). Inspector Pass asked for time to pay, but was ordered to pay forthwith. The only concession he managed to extract from the magistrates was a series of complimentary remarks about his service in the neighbourhood.

Inspector (later Superintendent) Alfred Pass
Selly Oak
5th July, 1910

Alfred Pass went on to become a superintendent and served until 1934 when he retired, aged sixty-two.

The first intake

Until the turn of the century, applicants to the Worcestershire Constabulary who were found to be suitable following initial examination, were usually taken on as soon as they applied. On 15th March 1902, for the first time, trainee policemen were taken on in a group known as an intake. There were eight men and they were joined two days later by a ninth. A brief outline of their service is given below, a typical sample of the recruits of the time.

PC Albert William Daniel Askew, aged nineteen. He was 5'8", weighed eleven stones and was a native of Wednesbury. His previous employment was as an axle turner and he was single. He remained at the police headquarters until 29th April 1902, and commenced duty at Dudley on the 30th. He was dismissed on 14th November 1904, after a series of drunken incidents.

2. PC William Edwin Best, aged twenty-three. He was 5'9", weighed sixteen stones and was a native of Alvechurch. He was an asylum attendant and a single man. He later married Ethel Hayne, from Quinton, and they had two children. In 1911 he was promoted to sergeant. He was posted to Oldbury on 30th April 1902, and served at Beech Lanes, Tat Bank and Redditch. He retired on 19th August 1927, and died on 27th August 1957.

3. PC Charles Butler, aged thirty. He was 5'11", weighed fourteen stones and seven pounds, and was a native of Broadway. He was formerly a compositor and was married to Florence Bearcroft of Offenham. They had two children. He was posted to Shrawley on 5th May 1902, and later served at Clows Top, Newnham Bridge, Rock and Oldbury, where he was a plain clothes officer. He retired on 14th March 1928.

4. PC John Edward Jennings, aged twenty-one. He was 5'9", weighed twelve stones and was a native of Rock. He was a labourer and a single man. He was posted to Bromsgrove on 30th April 1902, and was dismissed on 6th August 1903.

5. PC Walter Kennard, aged twenty-seven. He was 5'11", weighed twelve stones and was a native of St George's, Worcester. He had served in the Worcestershire Regiment as a musician for thirteen years. In 1907 he married Mary Avery of Worcester and they had one daughter. He was posted to Hay Mills on 30th April 1902, and served at Harvington until he was dismissed on 20th December 1911.

6 PC William Leonard Mann, aged twenty. He was 5'9", weighed twelve stones and was a native of Iverley near Stourbridge. He was a labourer and had served in the South Staffordshire Militia before purchasing his discharge. He married Katherine Lancaster of Acocks Green and they had one son. He was posted to Acocks Green on 30th April 1902, and served at Evesham and Fladbury before retiring on 31st July 1928.

7. PC Solomon Nash, aged twenty. He was 5'10", weighed twelve stones and was a native of Stoke Prior. He was a striker and a single man. On 30th April 1902, he was posted to Oldbury and later served at Kings Norton until he was dismissed on 19th October 1903 for drunkenness.

8. PC James Phillips, aged twenty. He was 6'0", weighed thirteen stones and four pounds, and was a native of St Michael's, Tenbury. He was a labourer, and in 1909 married Alice Glover of Moseley. He was posted to Great Witley on 30th April 1902, and served at Stourport, Kings Heath, Oldbury, Rounds Green, Sidemoor, Blackwell and Rednal, until he retired on 13th April 1929.

9. PC Arthur Harry Wall, aged twenty-one. He was 5'8", weighed twelve stones and three pounds, and was a native of Kingswinford. He joined the force on 17th March 1902. He was formerly a groom and married Florence Stanton of Stourbridge in 1907. They had one daughter. He was promoted to the rank of sergeant in 1910. He was posted to Kings Heath on 30th April 1902, and served at Oldbury, Rounds Green, Evesham and Blockley before retiring on 31st December 1929.

Almost two decades and a World War passed before the losses of policemen for disciplinary matters were substantially reduced.

PART III

Chapter Seven

Death of Lieutenant Colonel Carmichael

On Thursday 29th January 1903, the chief constable, Lieutenant Colonel George Lyndoch Carmichael, died at his home in Upper Wick at the age of seventy-one. He was buried at Astwood Cemetery in Worcester on Monday 2nd February 1903. He had served the county for more than thirty years.

The deputy chief constable, James Wasley, took over the reins of the force until a successor to Carmichael could be appointed. Wasley was a short, slightly built man who had joined the force in 1875 at the age of twenty-one. He had previously worked as a gamekeeper at Ragley Hall near Alcester and was married with four children.

Tributes to Carmichael filled the pages of local newspapers. The *Berrows Worcester Journal* reported that he had pursued his daily duties with energy and devotion until seven days before he died. As courts sat, magistrates around the county expressed their sympathies to their local superintendents. Superintendent Francis Pitt of Bromsgrove observed, "He was a strict disciplinarian" but "no one could be more kind to his men". Superintendent Alfred Pugh of Stourbridge commented, "Every officer in the force would be deeply grieved at his death, for he had always been a kind friend to every member of the force." Superintendent William Cope of Evesham had served under "the colonel' for twenty-eight years". During that time he had "never heard him use a cross word." The feelings of ordinary policemen, at the loss of their chief constable, were not recorded. Perhaps they had expressed their views a few years before, at the time of the Henry Kemp incident. At that time, Carmichael had been given a tremendous vote of confidence by his men.

A new broom

Lieutenant Colonel Herbert Sutherland Walker was selected as the new chief constable and he took up his post on 4th April 1903. Walker was thirty-eight years old with a distinguished army service record behind him. He was formerly of the Cameronians and had served with distinction in the West African Campaigns. He was the son of the Surgeon General, W. Walker of the Indian Medical Service and was educated at Rugby, Sandhurst and Cambridge. In 1897 he was part of an expedition to the Gold Coast where he was 'Mentioned in Dispatches' and later promoted to lieutenant colonel. At the turn of the century he was seconded to the Intelligence Division of the War Office.

Lt. Col. Herbert Sutherland Walker CBE
Chief Constable of the Worcestershire Constabulary
1903 - 1931

The new chief constable was keen to improve the professional knowledge of his men. He quickly set up regular periods of training in law and police procedures, followed by drill instruction. Walker insisted that his superintendents spent at least an hour each week training their subordinates. He judged each of them on the success of their instruction. As time progressed, these gatherings were used to pay the men their wages and became known as 'pay parades'.

As with any new broom, Walker issued instructions like confetti. They were circulated in the form of general orders and distributed so as to be available to all officers. Each directive was carefully copied into a book, kept for that purpose, before being passed on for the process to be repeated at the next station.

Walker's influence reached the ears of the civil servants at the Home Office. In 1907 a German government representative was advised that Worcestershire was one of the best rural police administrations to visit. When he had studied the force procedures the German visitor declared he would like to see the county's police systems implemented in Germany.

Motor cars

In 1903 the government introduced the Motor Car Act, which was designed to bring some sort of order to the increasing volume of motor traffic appearing on the roads. County councils were required to establish motor vehicle licensing departments and were responsible for the registration of motor vehicles. There was a fee of 20/- (£1.00) to register a motor car and 5/- (25p) to register a motorcycle. Drivers of these vehicles could obtain a driving licence annually at a cost of 5/- (25p), but the need to pass a driving test was still many years away.

Each city and county, and certain boroughs, were allocated one or more registrations, which comprised one or two letters to which a number could be added. Worcestershire was allocated four groups of registration letters, namely AB, NP, UY and WP. Worcester City received FK and Dudley FD. This system continued with adjustments until September 2001, when a different format was introduced.

The first vehicle registration mark to be issued in Worcestershire was AB 1 and it was allocated to a 5 h.p. Wolsley on 19th May 1903. The Wolsley was registered to 'Lieutenant Colonel Herbert Sutherland Walker, Worcs Police, The Cross House, Powick.' The motor car was used by the chief constable for both private and official purposes, although it was said that Walker walked from his home to his office in Castle Street each day.

The registration number was transferred to each of the chief constable's official motor cars until 1931 when it was taken out of circulation. For some time Lloyd Williams, who succeeded Walker as Chief Constable in 1931, used his own registration number EP 5056. In the meantime the Local Taxation Officer was bombarded with applications asking for AB 1 to be allocated to other vehicles. Each request was politely refused. On 28th September 1960 the registration number was re-issued to the chief constable's official motor car, which was, at that time, a 3781cc Jaguar. Today the registration mark continues to be used on the official car of the chief constable of the West Mercia Constabulary and its nominal value is included in the assets of the force.

Road accidents

The growth in road traffic, coupled with very poor driving standards, led to an increase in collisions. It fell to the police to establish the causes of these road accidents, identify breaches of the law and, in appropriate cases, report details of fatalities to the coroner. The independent nature of the police investigation was soon recognised by motor insurers. They began to apply for copies of police accident reports, known as abstracts, in order to settle their claims. At this time, policemen recorded all details in their pocket notebooks rather than on specially designed forms. Making copies of the contents of notebooks created additional clerical work, which eventually led, in 1909, to the force imposing a charge of 1/- (5p) for the provision of an abstract.

Young offenders and poor children

In 1908 the law changed to allow, for the first time, juvenile offenders - youngsters aged seven to fifteen - to be dealt with by juvenile courts. This departure from the existing law was a major step forward in dealing with young criminals. Previously, children had been dealt with by adult courts and routinely received adult sentences.

Many of the offending children came from impoverished families, or, in some cases, were abandoned to fend for themselves. Policemen saw at first hand the living conditions that these youngsters had to endure. There was little they could do to help until, in 1908, the Police Aided Boot Fund was introduced. For the next four decades, there were few police stations in the county that did not display a clearly marked, little wooden box on the front counter. Donations were made by police officers and the public, with the proceeds used to buy shoes, boots, or sometimes clothing, for less fortunate children.

Public counters

Early police stations made no provision for visits by the public. Indeed, visitors to police cottages were likely to be invited into the kitchen, or living room where there was one. Larger police stations sometimes had rooms where policemen gathered to prepare and eat their food or to deal with their paperwork, but these were not intended for visits from members of the public. As new main stations were built, around the turn of the century, rooms where the telephones were installed became focal points. Messages and other circulations were filed in this room, which was manned by a policeman known as an office reserve. Soon the public were admitted to this office area and, in due course, a wooden counter, desk or bookshelves were positioned close to the public entrance. It was over this furniture that business was conducted.

A commission of enquiry

Walker hardly had time to get his feet under his desk before being confronted with a situation at Sparkhill that was already getting out of hand because of misleading rumours. The superintendent at Sparkhill was Francis Pitt. He had been stationed there for just three months. Pitt, it was alleged, had birched two youths named Bertie Heekes and Ralph Taylor to extract confessions from them. Whilst it was not unusual for the police to birch offenders following their conviction at court, it was quite improper to do so for any other reason. The rumours got as far as the House of Commons, and Sir Walter Foster (MP for Derbyshire, Ilkeston) asked the Home Secretary if there would be an enquiry into the matter. The Home Secretary replied by expressing his satisfaction with the way that the chief constable was dealing with the incident.

The allegations stemmed from the arrest of the two youths on 3rd July 1904, for theft. They were taken to Sparkhill police station where Heekes admitted his part in the crime. He asked that he be birched as an alternative to being charged with the offence. This was done and, at some point in the proceedings, Taylor was in a position to physically attack his associate for admitting the offence. This resulted in a struggle as police officers tried to separate them. Superintendent Pitt was in the thick of the fray, and when Taylor was prevented from beating Heekes he turned his attentions to Pitt, kicking and punching him, whilst emitting a stream of abuse. Pitt, who later admitted losing his self-control, gave Taylor a good flogging.

Word soon got out about the incident, and the chief constable set up a commission of enquiry to get to the bottom of the matter. He was joined as chairman by three members of the police authority. Pitt meanwhile encouraged each of the police witnesses to give evidence that was favourable to him. By the time the commission of enquiry completed its work, Pitt had been sacked for telling lies, as were PC Arthur Drew and PC James Dumbleton. Two other policemen had their wages reduced for up to two years.

There was good work too

Although the wages of the Worcestershire policemen had once more fallen behind those of the surrounding forces, moral remained at a reasonable level, with reports of good work regularly arriving at headquarters from all parts of the county.

PC John Henry Green was on duty in George Street, Redditch at about 10.00p.m. on 28th October 1908. He was checking the security of a local pawnbroker's premises when he saw three men on the roof, removing slates. As soon as they realised they had been spotted the men began to run along the roof towards an adjoining yard. PC Green was able to climb a high wall and apprehend one of the three, but the others made good their escape. The descriptions of these men were circulated by telephone. During the early hours of the following morning, PC John Griffin was patrolling at Longbridge when he saw two men who were similar in appearance to the descriptions. It was said that he used considerable tact in effecting the arrest of both men. PC Green was awarded a merit badge and £2.0.0d, whilst PC Griffin was rewarded with £1.0.0d.

During the early evening of 14th November 1908, PC Edward McDonaugh was keeping observations in the Robin Hood golf pavilion at Hall Green. After about an hour, the door to the premises was forced and two men entered. One was carrying a lighted bicycle lamp and the other a weapon of some sort. The officer tackled both men and was severely beaten. The men were able to get away, but were later arrested. PC McDonaugh was given a reward of £2.0.0d and a merit badge.

At Upton upon Severn on 9th November 1908, PC Thomas Probert was on duty when he saw a horse drawing a wagon, galloping towards him. A man had already tried to stop it without success. The officer removed some children who were in the path of the animal, before standing in the roadway to face the animal. As the horse and wagon passed him, he seized the bridle rein and was dragged along the road for some distance before bringing the animal to a halt. PC Probert received a reward of £2.0.0d and a merit badge.

A mounted branch

In 1909 the Home Office urged the chief constable to establish a mounted branch to be used at times of "special emergency". The circular continued, "The value of mounted police when dealing with actual rioters and in breaking up a crowd, which if left, could become tumultuous is well recognised." Walker did not believe that there was a need to set up a full-time mounted branch. His predecessor had already made an ad hoc arrangement in which six policemen with experience of riding horses in the armed services were provided with saddles and harness. Horses were hired for their use as and when required. The Home Office circular prompted the SJC to increase the part-time mounted police numbers to twelve and allow them to continue to operate on a part-time basis, as before. The policemen who were selected included PC William Cooper and PC Alexander Moss. The mounted men were spread across the force and were used for all sorts of duties, not just crowd control. They regularly appeared at the Pershore races and, from time to time, at Pitchcroft in Worcester for the variety of events that were held there. In 1900, PC Cooper provided a mounted escort to the 3rd

78   From Fruit Trees to Furnaces - A History of the Worcestershire Constabulary

Worcestershire Regiment, which was marching from Worcester to Droitwich. Unfortunately, on his return he was somewhat worse for drink and was spotted in that condition in Fernhill Heath by Deputy Chief Constable Wasley. It cost him a fine of £5.0.0d and a severe reprimand, but he remained a mounted man and was still occasionally employed in those duties ten years later.

PC William Cooper from Kings Heath on mounted duty at Pershore Races on 2nd May, 1910

Early in 1915 the War Office asked for volunteers from the mounted policemen in the force to join the Military Mounted Police. The police committee authorised the enlistment of five policemen, but in the event only four joined up. They were PC John Lovejoy, PC Walter Jones, PC Roger Bullock and PC Edward Round. Although not officially recorded, this was probably the beginning of the end of the mounted branch. It is not mentioned again in any official documentation.

Election time at Droitwich

In 1910 a general election was held. Polling days were always difficult times for the police. Different factions were, more often than not, inclined to violence to impose their will or intimidate voters. It was not unusual for elections to be staggered over a number of days, to enable the police to deploy sufficient numbers of officers, at different locations, to maintain order. At Droitwich, feelings ran high during the count, as rumours circulated that the Tory candidate, the Hon. J.C. Lyttleton, was about to defeat the Liberal candidate. Many locals worked in the salt industry, or trades dependant upon it, and there was a fear that a political change in the area could lead to job losses.

James Wasley
Deputy Chief Constable
1900 - 1921

A large crowd of people, estimated by some to be a thousand strong, began a march through the town, causing mayhem as they went. The Tory offices were damaged, as were other suspected Tory strongholds, the Worcestershire Hotel and the Wagon and Horses public house. The damage caused to the town was considerable, and although there were extra policemen on duty they were overwhelmed by the mob. At about midnight the authorities decided that the 'Riot Act' should be read and the Mayor of Droitwich, Councillor Gabb, stepped forward. Shouting at the top of his voice he began to read the prescribed text, by the light of a candle held by the deputy chief constable James Wasley. Some reports claim that the candle was put out by a flying stone, but, whatever happened, the address was not heard in complete silence as the law required. An hour later the police cleared the streets, making some arrests.

A few weeks later, twelve of the rioters appeared at the Worcestershire Assizes. Mr Wasley declared to the court that he had never seen "…so evil disposed and persistent crowd…" in his thirty-four years as a policeman. Other witnesses gave evidence of the incident being very "good humoured" at times. At the end of a two-day hearing the defendants were found "not guilty" and were discharged.

Birmingham expands - again

By 1910 the cost of running the force was £46,500 per annum. This included a contribution of £16,000 from the government, which covered half of the cost of police pay and uniforms. The strength of the force stood at 463, but it was based on the 1901 census showing 488,355 residents. It was generally acknowledged that this figure was no longer accurate. The northern portion of the county had experienced a considerable increase in population, and the police to population ratio of 1 to 997 was now out of date. To ease the situation the chief constable made application to the police authority for a substantial increase in men.

As the authority pondered the application they were overtaken by events. Twenty years after its initial foray into the county, the city of Birmingham was seeking further expansion. On 9th November 1911, Yardley and Northfield divisions were transferred to Birmingham. Over one hundred Worcestershire policemen were retained in these districts by the Birmingham force to enable it to adjust to its increase in size. Some of these men were on temporary loan but, when the dust had settled, eighty-six county policemen remained in Birmingham.

The upheaval that the transfer caused to the county police also provided benefits in the running of the force. The introduction of the Police (Weekly Rest Day) Act, 1910, had placed an obligation upon police authorities in England and Wales to provide their police officers with fifty-two days off each year. This amounted to a day off each week. The pressures created by the Act were considerable and required creative management in most forces. Worcestershire, however, had the benefit of more than forty fully trained policemen who, when released from Birmingham, could be posted to locations where the need was greatest.

Many police authorities tried to reduce the impact of the rest days by including annual leave in the overall number of days off. This was not in the spirit of the legislation and the chief constable was careful to steer the authority away from that idea. He felt it would be unpopular, and would make it difficult for policemen and their families to visit family and friends in other parts of the country. He did hold the view, however, that annual holidays could be reduced.

A close call

Most police officers will say that police work is generally routine, interrupted occasionally by moments of excitement and danger. This was the situation when PC Harry King answered the telephone at Halesowen police station at about 12.45p.m. on 4th May 1911. He was told that a Russian Jew, Israel Chyim Levenstein, was walking down the Midland Railway line, from Northfield towards Hunnington. He was brandishing a loaded revolver and threatening to shoot anyone who came close to him. A small group of people, including policemen, had gathered and was pursuing him at a sensible distance. PC King joined PC William Berry and they began walking up the railway line in search of Levenstein. They found him near to Illey Bridge, trapping him between themselves and the group following him. As they approached, he pointed the revolver at them and shouted "Keep away or I'll shoot you." King and Berry allowed him to pass and joined the following party. One person in the group had a revolver, which he handed to PC King, who immediately hurried after Levenstein, ordering him to stop. The man turned and pointed his revolver at the policeman and said, "Stand back, take one more step nearer and I will kill you, as I want to kill myself. Now leave me alone."

**PC's William Berry and Harry King following the presentations
of their King's Police Medals on 22nd July, 1911**

The gunman left the railway line and climbed over a fence into Illey Lane. As he did so the officer made a grab for him but was unable to hold him. The man then began to make his way down the lane, with PC King following, trying to get closer and closer. Levenstein turned suddenly and fired his gun at King, at point blank range. The bullet passed close to the policeman's head and left him stunned for a few moments. King tried to fire his revolver but it misfired. As Levenstein took aim for a second time PC Berry, who was close by, charged at him. This caused the gunman to turn and fire at him, aiming at his head. Again he missed. PC King then fired his gun at Levenstein, but also missed. Berry grabbed the gunman around the waist and they both fell to the ground. There was a violent struggle in which Levenstein held his gun to Berry's chest. Before he was able to fire, a young man named William Redding seized the gunman by the throat and jerked him backwards, a movement which no doubt saved the policeman's life. PC King was then able to help handcuff Levenstein, who was removed to the police station.

Each policemen received a reward of £3.0.0d and a merit badge. Later they were awarded the King's Police Medal, and the Carnegie Hero Fund Trust gave each of them a £5.0.0d reward. William Redding received a reward of £2.0.0d.

Sadly, William Berry was dismissed from the force in 1912 and his medal was forfeited in 1913.

Chapter Eight

Changes in transport

In the early years of the twentieth century, wages for most policemen were insufficient to buy motor cars. Many of them had bicycles and some had motorcycles. Whichever machine they had, the chances were that it had been purchased with a loan.

Within the police force there was mounting concern at the high number of bicycle accidents involving policemen. They were being injured both on and off duty, some quite seriously. As a consequence, the use of pedal cycles by constables was severely restricted. Sergeants and inspectors, however, were permitted to ride cycles as and when they were required to do so. In 1910 the chief constable issued an order, that specifically forbade the use of pedal cycles when making conference points. The policemen showed their usual ingenuity when dealing with such instructions. There are many tales of the lengths to which they would go to avoid being caught using a cycle to get to a conference point or meet. One well used story tells of the constable who rushed on his bicycle to make a meet with his sergeant. He quickly hid the machine behind a hedge and confidently greeted his supervisor whilst sporting his bicycle clips.

**Superintendent Richard Beale and his groom
PC Alfred Bartlett in a police dog cart c1904**

Sergeants and inspectors knew the dodges and, after making the meet, often invited the poor PC to ride with them in the police cart. Sometimes they travelled many miles before being set down to continue their patrol, and recover their bicycle.

Although part of the reason for the rise in cycle accidents was the increased use of motor cars, Colonel Walker was eager to see his force join the motoring age. In November 1913 he dispatched his chauffeur, PC Thomas Timms, to a motor show in London. His mission was to inspect the cars on display, and gather as much information about them as he could.

On 3rd January 1914 the chief constable arrived at a Police Sub-Committee meeting, armed with facts and figures about motor cars. He intended to convince the committee members of the suitability of replacing the horses and traps, used by superintendents, with small motor cars.

Walker proposed that two motor cars be purchased initially, at a cost of no more than £300. The cars would be based at Bromsgrove and Pershore, the smallest and largest divisions in area respectively. He forecast that over a four-year term the use of motor cars would be significantly cheaper than the existing methods of transport.

The committee was satisfied that there was merit in his proposal and agreed to purchase two new motor cars at a cost of £280.3.0d (£280.15). The first was a two-cylinder 7 h.p. Swift. It was grey with green leather upholstery. The second was a black and green two-cylinder 8 h.p. Perry. Both vehicles were registered on 13th March 1914, as AB 3571 and AB 3572.

On 27th April 1915, the county police registered a further three, brand new Swifts for the use of superintendents at Malvern, Stourport and Stourbridge. They were each grey 7 h.p. vehicles, registered AB 4250, AB 4251 and AB 4252.

Unfortunately, inflation during the first world war completely destroyed the chief constable's carefully prepared operating expenses. Petrol costs went up sharply; so did tyres and oil prices. To ease the financial burden, he asked his superintendents to reduce their monthly mileage and to travel by train wherever possible. This proved to be insufficient, as expenditure on the motor cars continued to escalate. In 1918 he reluctantly had to apply to the police sub-committee for an increase in the annual motor car allowances for superintendents. In spite of these setbacks, overall the project was a success.

In March 1921 the chief constable drew the attention of the police sub-committee to the motor cars being used by the superintendents. The purchase of the cars had proved to be a sensible investment for the force. They had given good service for six or seven years, but the need to reduce the transport budget led the chief constable to suggest a different method of financing police transport in the future. He had discovered that some police forces gave their superintendents an allowance to run their own motor cars, and he felt that the idea was worthy of implementation in Worcestershire.

As a result of his proposal, it was agreed that when the current motor cars ceased to be economical to run, superintendents would be required to buy their own motor cars. They would receive an allowance of between £72 and £90 per annum. The exact figure would be decided according to the size of their divisions. In addition, the sum of up to £15 would be paid to cover car tax and insurance. Those superintendents who could not afford to buy a motor car would be granted an interest-free loan of up to £100.

**Superintendent Frank Jones and his driver PC Douglas Hebdige.
They are sitting in a Standard 9.5hp Rhyl motor car
which was probably owned by the Superintendent.
Bromsgrove c1923**

The question of disposal of the motor cars came up rather quickly. In February 1922 the cars were offered for sale to garages throughout the force area, with disappointing results. The chief constable did not receive an offer higher than £50. As a result, the cars were sold to superintendents for £50 each.

First World War

The latter part of July 1914 became a time of intense activity for the county police as the Home Office released a flood of instructions. In the event of an invasion or hostile landing by the Germans, the police should telegraph the nearest army command. Telegraph offices at Kidderminster and Redditch were instructed to remain open day and night to carry this and a host of other information. The police were to ensure that idle and disorderly women did not enter or loiter in the vicinity of barracks. The chief constable should identify a suitable location for a prisoner of war camp, sufficient to accommodate one thousand prisoners, one hundred guards and twelve administrative staff. The Home Office wished to know how many Germans, Austrians and Hungarians were registered as aliens in the county. The list of requests seemed endless.

Almost immediately, the routine of life for the county's policemen changed. Their responsibilities grew substantially as they were called upon to look after military and vulnerable installations. Those men who were away on leave were recalled to duty. The return of these officers was considered so important that the county offered to pay for the travel costs of the policemen and their families. In some cases the outward journey was paid for as well.

As mobilisation got under way, twenty-two policemen were included in the one hundred and thirty county council employees who went to war in 1914.

The departure of so many policemen at one time meant that the additional duties thrust upon the force weighed heavily with those who remained. The extra work was borne with good spirits, at first. The men lost much of their already limited free time and the chief constable soon had to reverse the order prohibiting the use of pedal cycles. Beats had, of necessity, been redefined and were just too big to patrol on foot.

Walker was required to take up his former role in military intelligence and, during his absences, the deputy chief constable took control of the force. This arrangement was put on a formal footing when the police sub-committee directed that from 1st June 1915, the deputy chief constable, James Wasley, would receive an additional sum of £100 per annum to cover the extra work and travelling his new duties required. The chief clerk, Superintendent William Farmer, received an extra £50 in recognition of the increase in his duties as well.

Some documents refer to the chairman of the county council, John Willis Bund, becoming the acting chief constable. This is not borne out by the minutes of the police authority meetings. However, Bund was an extremely forceful individual who was used to getting his own way. This was clearly illustrated in 1901 when he crossed swords with the then chief constable, Colonel Carmichael. At an SJC meeting, Bund made a derogatory remark concerning the police failing to prosecute farmers who paid their workmen with cider, in contravention of the Truck Act. Carmichael took exception to the comment and attempted to intervene to put forward his point of view. Bund would hear none of it and ordered him to leave the room. There continued a very heated exchange, which the chairman finally won when he managed to get the chief constable to "hold his tongue." In the circumstances, Wasley may have proved to be easier to intimidate than Walker. Whatever the situation was, the chief constable regularly presented his reports to the police authority.

John William Willis Bund was an extremely powerful character holding the chairmanship of the Worcestershire County Council, the Worcestershire Quarter Sessions, the Cardiganshire Quarter Sessions and the Severn Fishery Board, each for upwards of thirty years. He held formidable opinions on many subjects including teachers "They turn out vagabonds and little scoundrels" and policewomen, "It would be a great mistake having a lot of women, with very little to do, going about gossiping and saying they are policemen." Bund died in 1928 aged 85.

From Fruit Trees to Furnaces - A History of the Worcestershire Constabulary   87

John William Willis Bund c1920

By January 1915, eight police officers had been selected to serve in the army as drill instructors. Two of them, Sergeant William Poyner from Bewdley and Sergeant Frederick Smith from Blockley, were posted to Norton Barracks at Worcester. They trained soldiers during the week, and at the weekends they resumed their police duties at their stations. They were each paid 5/- (25p) for the journeys they made in connection with their military service.

PC (later Inspector) William Poyner Droitwich c1902

Sergeant (later Superintendent) Frederick Smith c1911

On 10th June 1915, twenty-three policemen resigned from the Worcestershire Constabulary to enlist in the services. A parade was organised at the Shirehall in Worcester as part of their send-off. The police authority allowed their colleagues a day's pay and return railway fares to attend. To ease the difficulties created by these departures, a number of men, of various ranks, who were due for retirement were asked to remain in post until the end of the war.

Early in 1915 the battlefield arrived on English soil when German airships made raids on the East Coast. In all, there were fifty-seven airship raids in which 564 people were killed and more than 1,300 injured. On January 31st 1916, the attacks got as far as the Midlands. Six or seven airships attacked, dropping bombs across midland counties, penetrating as far inland as the Black Country in Staffordshire. Although the effects of the raid were played down by the authorities through the government press bureau, citizens in the affected and adjoining areas felt extremely vulnerable.

Whilst Worcestershire did not suffer in these raids, their consequences on Staffordshire's industrial south were too close for comfort. The county council was outraged that the military authorities had not given any intimation of the raid to the police, even though information of it was available to them. This led to a meeting of Midlands civic leaders in Birmingham on 9th February. Between them they hammered out an agreement to ensure the efficient notification of imminent air attacks to Midlands police forces. Meanwhile, Acting Chief Constable James Wasley was congratulated by the county council for the "prompt and energetic precautions" he and his staff took at the time of the raid.

It could never be said that a policeman's pay was anything to write home about. Furthermore, his work increased as the war progressed, but his wages did not. The cost of living was growing at an alarming rate and many commodities were becoming scarce or impossible to obtain. Men and women in other occupations, particularly those connected with the war effort, could earn wages of more than £5 a week. The newest police recruit, on the other hand, was earning less than a quarter of that. In Worcestershire, policemen's wages were not even keeping pace with those in surrounding police forces. In 1915 the SJC made a slight upward adjustment to wages. The lowest-paid men then received £1.5.1d (£1.25) a week. Even after this wage review, a superintendent with more than ten years' service in the rank did not earn as much as a munitions worker.

In 1916, policemen were granted a weekly war bonus that took account of their circumstances, including marital status and number of dependant children. This bonus was regularly adjusted in a futile attempt to keep abreast of inflation. By July 1918, policemen were paid by the week instead of by the day. A constable earned up to £2.10.0d (£2.50) a week and a sergeant £2.18.0d (£2.90).

The war proved to have an insatiable appetite for personnel. Recruiting rules were constantly amended to absorb into the services those people previously excluded. A steady flow of police officers resigned from the force to take up arms. Some of them chose that route, having been convicted of breaches of discipline. The chief constable made it plain to them that by taking such a course of action they would avoid punishment.

In June 1916 the Superintendents of Dudley, Oldbury, Halesowen, Stourbridge, Bromsgrove and Stourport divisions were instructed to select up to twenty of their more capable and reliable special constables who were willing to volunteer for police duty. The selected men worked, in their spare time, with experienced policemen thereby ensuring, they would be suitably trained if their services were required. This was a huge demand upon the goodwill of the specials, who were not paid for their duties. At the year end, special constables were being deployed to beats in areas where the resident policeman had enlisted. Whatever duties they carried out, the specials were normally engaged in a manner that avoided interference with their paid occupations.

By November 1916, recruiting for the regulars was completely abandoned and the special constabulary came into its own. Spiralling costs, combined with clothing manufacturers dedicating their productions to military clothing, meant that few of them had a uniform to wear. Generally they worked in civilian clothing with only an arm band and badge to distinguish them.

As belts continued to be tightened, some of the population, especially country folk, tried to be as self-sufficient as possible. They grew their own vegetables, whilst having a few chickens scratching about in the back garden. The more ambitious kept a pig or two. The country bobby was no exception. Most rural stations had large gardens, and the occupants made sure they were fully utilised. The police authority and the chief constable tended to turn a blind eye to such resourcefulness, but when, in April 1918, Superintendent Thomas Hinde applied to build a pig sty at the main Stourbridge police station, close to the town centre, it was met with a firm refusal.

War or no war, police work still had to be done. PC Harry Gummery was the local policeman for Bredon. In August 1915, he was called to a burglary at the house of Martin Paget at Mill End, Bredon, in which a pair of boots, a shawl, a basket and food valued at 7/10d (39p) had been stolen. It transpired that the culprit was Ann Read, a fifty-eight-year-old homeless woman. PC Gummery arrested her at Bredon's Norton and began to walk her back towards Pershore police station, whilst at the same time pushing his bicycle. When they got to Eckington Bridge, Ann decided to take her leave and leaped into the river. Harry Gummery, who was a non-swimmer, immediately jumped in after her and managed to drag her to the side. They both arrived at Pershore, wet, but none the worse for the ordeal.

Coal stealing was a common offence, particularly in the Black Country. The coal was transported by canal to the factories in and around Dudley to fuel large furnaces. When the canal barges laden with coal were drawn up at wharves to be unloaded, they provided easy pickings for thieves, many of whom lived a hand to mouth existence during the war. The local coal merchants association was aware of the problem and displayed signs offering rewards of £20 for information leading to the conviction of offenders. On Wednesday September 25th 1918, PC Harry Pratley was on duty at Park Head, Woodside, Dudley when he saw four women stealing coal from a canal boat owned by the Stourbridge Glaze Brick Company. The women had gathered 1½ cwt (76 kilos) of coal, which was valued at 2/3d (12p). He arrested them, and five days later they were fined by Dudley magistrates.

PC Harry Pratley
Dudley c1911

In a report to the chief constable in which he claimed the reward of £20, PC Pratley drew attention to the arrests he had made. The application was quite inappropriate, but he did receive a reward of one guinea (£1.05). Harry Pratley should have known better. He had eleven years' service and was considered to be a good officer, but in January 1920 he was dismissed for being under the influence of drink and refusing to obey orders.

The return of peace – Demobilisation

The end of the war saw a steady stream of servicemen being demobilised. Former Worcestershire policemen were fortunate enough to return to their jobs, which had been held open. Once they had been sworn in again, most of them were posted back to their old stations, although many were moved on within a short time.

With vast numbers of men returning to the labour market there was a wealth of potential recruits for the police force. The administration staff at Worcester were overwhelmed with applications, which led to delays in dealing with the candidates. Some were able to gain an advantage because they knew someone in the force, or at least someone of some social standing, who could put in a good word for them.

Police Constable Frederick Hayes

Frederick Hayes was such an applicant. He had served in the Royal Field Artillery for four and a half years as a gun layer. The years of continuous concussion as the heavy artillery pieces were fired was to have a serious effect on his hearing in later years. He was discharged from the army on 5th February 1919, and wanted to join the police force, much against his mother's wishes. She had envisaged him taking up gardening or an associated occupation.

Fred's first port of call was Barnards Green police station at Malvern, where he spoke to PC Charles Clarke to find out about the force. They discussed the prospects of a career in the police force, which gave him the encouragement he needed to apply. As a result of their conversation he went to the county police headquarters in Castle Street, Worcester, where he met Sergeant George Hayes (no relation), the drill sergeant. Fred completed the application forms and went back home to await the call. More than a month went by, but he heard nothing. His army pay had finally run out and he was concerned about how he was going to manage. A visit to Sergeant Edwin Powell at Malvern did he trick. Within a few days, on 30th March 1919 he was asked to join the Worcestershire Constabulary. Frederick Hayes became Police Constable 10 and, at the age of twenty-two, was part of an intake of twelve men, all ex-servicemen.

PC Frederick Hayes
Halesowen
c1936

Post-war training for new recruits was still fairly basic. The billiard room at the police headquarters doubled as the classroom. Recruits sat around the billiard table, which was covered with a cloth to protect it. Each man was issued with a hardback book, with lined pages, in which he wrote out the chief constables orders, Home Office instructions and extracts of law describing his legal powers. The students would be tested on their knowledge, both in written and verbal examinations. Part of each afternoon was set aside for inspections and drill in the yard at the rear of headquarters. In the evenings the recruits patrolled on foot, either by themselves or with an experienced officer. The uniforms issued to them were invariably second-hand and required alteration, a task undertaken by a tailor who lived nearby. Each recruit was provided with three sets of uniform: one night, one day and one special. They had two helmets, two caps, four pairs of black woollen gloves and four pairs of white gloves.

Having completed his initial training, Fred Hayes filled a large metal trunk with his belongings and paid a man to push it on a trolley to the railway station in Foregate Street. He had been posted to Oldbury and travelled by train, arriving just in time to be caught up in the homeward-bound rush hour. He manhandled his trunk onto a packed tram and had to stand on the top deck as it clanked along. The journey was made in full uniform, with the metal plate on the top of his helmet striking against the roof of the tram as it rocked and lurched along the rails.

Young, single officers were often used to boost police numbers in country districts during the hop and pea picking seasons, when large influxes of land workers would move in. Invariably there were drunken brawls amongst the workers, as well as an increase in petty crime in the area. Many of the workers were gypsies who followed the agricultural and market gardening calendar around the country, but a substantial number were from the Black Country, spending their holidays in the country, picking the crops. The farmers normally provided very basic accommodation for the pickers, usually a barn or an outbuilding. Similarly, the local policeman would arrange lodgings for his visiting colleagues, but their standards varied enormously.

Frederick Hayes was not at Oldbury long before he was sent, temporarily, to Shelsley Beauchamp. He arrived, with his bicycle, at Kidderminster railway station, where a Shelsley farmer picked him and his bike up, in an Austin motor car. He was conveyed to his lodgings, which turned out to be so badly infested with fleas that he had to hang his uniform outside.

Later in his service, Fred became the driver for his superintendent, but only for a short time. The superintendent's car was without an efficient braking system and quite unroadworthy. A journey when the superintendent was driving was a terrifying experience. What was worse, if it could be, the senior officer's dog was taken everywhere in the car. Normal toilet training, for the dog, had never been achieved because it suffered a severe bladder problem. The smell that emanated from the vehicle, accompanied by the interest that it aroused in passing canines, made the job of superintendent's driver much less attractive than normal.

PC Harvey Haynes
Yardley
May 1910

A police union - but not for long

Early in 1919 a committee under Lord Desborough was set up to look at police pay and conditions in England, Wales and Scotland. At about the same time, a branch of the National Union of Police and Prison Officers was formed at Dudley. It boasted thirty-six members, including the secretary, PC Harvey Haynes. A small number of policemen at Stourbridge also joined, but there was little interest elsewhere in the county. The group quickly advised the chief constable and Chief Superintendent Speke of Dudley that they had no complaints to make about their treatment.

The Desborough Committee report recommended improvements in the pay and conditions of police officers, and when they were implemented Worcestershire police wages almost doubled overnight.

Policemen at Dudley and Redditch got to hear that, in some police forces, officers who had served throughout the war were to be financially compensated for lost leave. They applied to the chief constable to be granted similar remuneration. At a subsequent police committee meeting, Colonel Walker announced his intention to allow all ranks who had served in the force during the war to have an additional seven days' annual leave. He then recommended that the applications for payment should be rejected by the committee, which they were.

The chief constable then drafted a reply to the men of the Dudley and Redditch divisions, in his unusual Victorian third-party style. He was barely able to conceal his anger. "...the chief constable feels bound to say that he is very surprised at receiving the petition and cannot help thinking that the men did not fully realise the circumstances." Walker then proceeded to describe the generosity of the county in awarding the recent pay rise two months early. He mentioned the many thousands of men who had not only given up their leave but had given their lives during the war. He closed by commenting on the impression the public would be given "...that there are some members of the Worcestershire police, who grudge any curtailment of their privileges, even when their country is fighting for its existence, unless they are paid for it."

By the middle of 1919 the National Union of Police and Prison Officers had become more militant. The Dudley branch agreed that, although its members would not strike, they did not wish to be drafted into other districts where policemen were on strike. In a report to the chief constable, they asked for eight grievances to be sympathetically dealt with. In accordance with government policy, Walker declined to respond to their correspondence. He had already circulated a report in which he reiterated the government position; any police officer who went on strike would be deemed to have tendered his resignation.

A police strike was finally called on 31st July 1919. Locally, 119 Birmingham policemen responded, but when the strike collapsed they were all dismissed and no-one was reinstated. No policemen from Worcestershire were involved and none was used to supplement the shortages caused by striking policemen in other areas. On 4th August 1919, Dudley policemen Frederick Allen, Frederick James and Eli Stafford were approached by five Birmingham policemen who were on strike. They were each encouraged to support the police strike, which the Birmingham men claimed was supported by many other trade unions. The Dudley men declined.

The introduction of the Police Act of 1919, in August of that year, led to the demise of the Dudley branch of the union. The secretary, Harvey Haynes, reported the resignation en-bloc of all the members on 10th September 1919.

The last execution at Worcester gaol

Djang Djin Sung was convicted of the murder of his fellow countryman Zee Ming Wu in what came to be known as the Warley Woods murder. Zee Ming Wu had been reported missing from his lodgings on 23rd June 1919, and was known to have the sum of £240 in his post office savings book. The savings book turned up the next day at a post office in London. The post office official was not happy about the signature and, when questioned, the Chinese man who had presented it left the building hurriedly, leaving the savings book behind. Wu's body was eventually found in Warley Woods. After protracted enquiries, Sung was arrested in London for an assault on another Chinese man. He quickly became a suspect for the Warley murder. He alleged that another man was responsible for the murder and theft, but this was proved to be false. On 3rd December 1919, Sung was the last person to be executed at Worcester gaol.

Chapter Nine

Dudley

When the Worcestershire Constabulary was formed in 1839, Dudley, although isolated in south Staffordshire, was part of the county, but did not wish to be included in the county policing plan. The Dudley Town Commissioners, who were the ruling authority from 1791 until 1852, had powers of their own to appoint constables. Although they had received at least one deputation from the local citizens, asking for the introduction of night constables, nothing was done until 1827 when four inadequate watchmen were employed.

The commissioners were faced with many difficulties when they took office. The town's streets were unnamed and houses were not numbered. The accumulated filth and lack of street lighting made movement on foot, particularly at night, something of a skill. Worst of all, the sanitary conditions were dreadful, with inadequate fresh water, leading to serious epidemics. Allegedly, 70% of Dudley's inhabitants died before they were twenty years old. A combination of laxity, inadequate resources, and insufficient powers on the part of the commissioners meant that the situation was slow to change.

As late as 1840 the commissioners were resisting the creation of a police force, determined to operate with two constables, Joseph Jewkes and Henry Smitheman, and nine watchmen. Indeed, in an effort to avoid a rate-supported police force, one hundred prominent citizens formed an association offering rewards leading to the prosecution of felons; a scheme designed to protect themselves and their property.

In 1845 the county took over the policing of the town. When Dudley became a borough in 1865 it was legally required to provide and pay for a police force of its own. The county police committee was eager to maintain the status quo and quickly approached the Dudley authorities with a proposition. It anticipated that Dudley would agree to a similar arrangement to that already in place with the Borough of Evesham in which the borough would be policed as part of the county. What eventually emerged was a unique agreement in which the borough retained the purse strings for the policing in Dudley, but the chief constable was responsible for administration and personnel. The unfortunate consequences of this arrangement could not have been foreseen.

The borough council set up a watch committee to look after the borough force and to keep the council appraised of police activities. It was a similar arrangement to that operating in the county, with the police committee reporting to the Worcestershire Court of Quarter Sessions.

The watch committee decided that it wanted its policemen to be different from the main county force, both in uniform and structure. Advertisements were placed in the *Dudley Guardian* and the *Dudley Herald* newspapers, inviting local tailors to tender for the uniform contract. There was no suitable contractor in Dudley to make the hats and they were purchased elsewhere. When the helmet plates were manufactured the watch committee insisted that they bore the borough rather than the county arms.

The Dudley Fire Brigade was staffed by Dudley policemen. Only two civilian personnel were employed: the engineer and the driver of the horse-drawn engine. Although they were civilians, there is evidence that they were sometimes dressed in old police uniform to make up the numbers. The brigade captain was the chief superintendent, with some of the subordinate ranks appointed to other fire brigade roles. However, in later years, the post of captain of the fire brigade was occasionally held by sergeants.

The fire-fighting equipment used by the brigade was of poor quality and badly maintained. Two police fire-fighters found this out to their cost in 1887 when their scaling ladder broke and they fell to the ground. Their injuries made them unavailable for both their police and fire brigade duties. In another incident, in 1889, PC/Fireman William White was sent to a fire at the timber yard of Roberts and Cooper at Brierley Hill. A twenty-feet-high wall collapsed on him and fractured his left leg. He was off duty for 170 days. Even when he returned to work he was only fit enough for reserve duty, confining him to the police station for a further period. The loss of this man from his normal duties was frustrating enough, but the real rub was the fact that the fire was in Staffordshire, not Worcestershire.

Dudley Police Station c1918
Inspector Harry Miles and PC Harry Haggett
pose with Chief Superintendent Speke

Successive chief constables could never come to terms with the fire brigade duties undertaken by their officers because they felt constrained by the situation. The Dudley policemen/firemen earned extra money and had additional pension rights. Moving them routinely to another part of the force could result in financial hardship for the individual and his family, whilst the force was faced with the additional costs for kitting them out with a new uniform and equipment. In times of disturbance, accompanied by fire, the force was immediately depleted by the loss of the firemen. This meant that policemen had to be brought in from elsewhere in the force. The newcomers were easily identified because of the difference in uniform and were singled out by local troublemakers. The assaults on non-Dudley personnel were frequent because the offenders took advantage of the unfortunate circumstances that the visiting policemen found themselves in.

The first chief of police at Dudley was Superintendent Joseph Jewkes. He had been a local constable in the town for many years and joined the force at the age of thirty-nine. In 1857 he was found to be unable to perform his duties because of his age and ill health. In one of his characteristic displays of compassion, Harris persuaded the police authority to keep Jewkes on the books as a nominal constable until he had completed fifteen years' service, thus enabling him to draw a pension.

Henry Burton replaced Jewkes and was appointed chief superintendent. The rank of the senior officer at Dudley was an early source of friction between the county and borough authorities. The watch committee insisted that the chief officer should be a chief superintendent. Apart from this being a departure from the Home Office instructions on the subject, it once again put Dudley out of step with the rest of the force, where divisions were commanded by superintendents.

When Dudley became a borough, Burton's position became extremely difficult. He was required to serve two masters: the chief constable and the watch committee. Both were very exacting, often issuing incompatible instructions. Nevertheless, Burton skilfully kept the chief constable appraised of the activities of the watch committee, whilst generally maintaining cordial relations with the borough authorities.

Henry Burton had suffered insanitary living conditions at Stourbridge and he was not to be free of them when he moved to Dudley. In August 1873, he reported that the water supply from the well in the police yard was tainted and the wellbeing of the police families who lived nearby was suffering considerably. A sample of the water was sent to the county analyst who discovered that it contained a high concentration of iron. He reported that it was totally unsuitable for household use and pointed out that there was a strong possibility of health problems for those who drank it. As a short-term measure, a barrel of fresh water was placed in the police yard for all to use, but within two years the South Staffordshire Water Company was providing water to the police quarters in Priory Street.

Economy was the watchword for the Dudley authorities. Throughout its association with the Worcestershire police force, the council allocated unrealistic funds to the watch committee, for police purposes. In its turn, the watch committee tried to trim the budget further whenever it could. This was highlighted at Netherton police station, which was leased from three local businessmen, Messrs. Higgs, Walker and Hotchkiss, with a condition that the building was maintained by the borough.

In January 1873, the owners wrote to Chief Superintendent Burton to express their concern about the deterioration of their building. Burton passed the letter to the watch committee, which proceeded to take a series of measures to defer the need for a decision on the matter. First it directed the clerk to write to the county to 'clarify' the position. The reply stated that it was the watch committee's responsibility to keep the premises in good repair and to get on with it. Next, it formed a sub-committee comprising two committee members and the borough surveyor. The sub-committee probably did not meet and it certainly did not report.

Nine months after the first letter an exasperated Mr Hotchkiss wrote once more. He pointed out that the condition of the premises was having a detrimental affect upon its value. He now insisted that the conditions of the lease be complied with. The clerk to the watch committee wrote back to say that the matter was under consideration and the work would be carried out shortly. The letter also bemoaned the committee's difficult financial position, explaining that the work would have been carried out sooner were it not for the council's problems. The records do not show if the matter was ever satisfactorily resolved, but it was certainly a sign of things to come.

In 1877, tenders were invited from local decorators to paint the police cells. Three quotations were considered: £14.0.0d, £13.0.0d and £7.10.0d (£7.50). The committee chose the latter, from John Higgs of King Street, Dudley. One would have expected alarm bells to have sounded when such disparate bids were submitted, but the committee subsequently offered Higgs further work.

At its meeting on Monday 22nd February 1875, the watch committee ordered the installation of one gas light in each of the police cottages in Priory Road. Residents were instructed that the lights had to be extinguished by midnight each evening, on the grounds of economy.

In 1876 the committee became concerned that members of the public could see the necks and shirts of Dudley policemen above the collars of their uniform. An order was given for each officer to wear a piece of leather, known as a stock, below the hook and eye fastening of the tunic's collar. Aside from the discomfort this caused the men, the measure set them further apart from their county colleagues.

The early part of 1892 saw government pressure being brought to bear upon the watch committee, which was responsible for the conduct of the Dudley Police superannuation fund. The fund contained £3,740.1.4d (£3,740.07) and legally it had to be transferred into the coffers of the county superannuation fund. A meeting on the subject, held at Dudley on 27th January 1892, was reported back to the chief constable by Chief Superintendent Henry Burton. He said, "…some, perhaps the majority were for keeping the fund in the Bank of the Corporation, but nothing was definitely arrived at…".

In February, the Secretary of State wrote to the Dudley Corporation. He required the authority to explain why the legal requirement for the superannuation funds to be amalgamated had not been fulfilled. The town clerk, Mr Warmington, replied giving an exaggerated account of the actions that were being undertaken by the corporation to finalise the agreement. Home office officials realised that very little was happening and their response was blunt. If the matter was not settled as speedily as possible then the government grant was at risk and may not be paid before the end of the financial year. Within two days the watch committee met and agreed to transfer the funds.

The discipline records of the force indicate that, prior to the First World War, drunkenness amongst policemen was a serious problem. In Dudley it was far worse than anywhere else in the county, in fact it merited particular attention by the chief constable. In 1905 Walker became aware of a wave of housebreakings in the borough. He decided that the way to deal with them was to extend the daily working hours of the Dudley policemen.

In December 1906 the watch committee got to hear that a substantial number of local policemen had been disciplined for misconduct, by the chief constable. The committee asked the chief constable for an explanation. Walker told the members that in the previous three and a half years he had received thirty-six reports of serious misconduct involving twenty-three borough policeman. The total police strength for Dudley was forty-eight men. Whilst a considerable improvement in standards had occurred elsewhere in the force during the preceding three years, an analysis of the problems at Dudley revealed that they were due almost entirely to alcohol consumption. The practice that prevailed in Dudley, of standing drinks to officers both on and off duty, lay at the root of the difficulties. Walker explained that there was a serious temptation to young officers who, in many cases, were unwilling to give offence to influential persons by refusing to accept the offer of a drink, which was intended as a generous gesture.

The chief constable was able to produce details of the twenty-three Dudley officers, including Inspector George Wainwright, an alcoholic, who had to be moved to Droitwich. He resigned a year later because of alcoholism and being in debt. Sergeant Thomas Harris was dismissed after a number of instances involving drink. He too was an alcoholic. One of his colleagues, Sergeant George Andrews, was moved to Lye and later demoted, whilst Sergeant William Cooper was reduced in rank and later moved to Beech Lanes. Cooper must have been well regarded because, in spite of a poor disciplinary record, he managed to regain his rank after about eighteen months.

Many constables stationed at Dudley were also affected. One committed suicide, four were dismissed, three were ordered to resign, eleven were either reduced in pay or class, four were fined and five reprimanded. Two officers took sick leave.

On 3rd February 1907, seventeen constables from Dudley presented a petition to their chief superintendent, Richard Speke. It asked that the chief constable re-instate their eight-hour working day. The men felt that the longer shifts were responsible for a lot of sickness and were definitely causing difficulties at home. Colonel Walker agreed to their request, but reminded the men that the reason for the increase in hours was to combat a spate of burglaries that were allowed to get out of hand because the officers had concentrated more on their drinking than their duties.

Decades of bickering between the county and borough authorities reached a critical state in 1913 following the inspection of the force by Her Majesties Inspector of Constabulary. The borough ratio of population to each policeman was considerably higher than the national average because the watch committee had consistently refused to finance an increase in police numbers. The national average stood at one constable to eight hundred of the population, whilst Dudley stood at one to one thousand. For this reason and the fact that the police accommodation was totally unsatisfactory, the Home Office refused to issue a certificate of efficiency for the force. This was a serious matter, not just for Dudley but for the whole county, as a substantial part of the organisation's finances was obtained from government sources.

The decision should have come as no surprise to the Borough Council, as successive Inspectors of Constabulary had been critical over a number of years about the state of the buildings, both for the police families and for prisoners. Much of the accommodation occupied by the police families had been condemned on a number of occasions. The warnings had been consistently ignored.

The Home Office decision placed the SJC in an impossible situation. The remainder of the county would be suffering for circumstances that were totally outside its control.

Meanwhile the watch committee reacted in a completely predictable way by stating the matter was under consideration. This verbal smoke screen, designed to create an impression of activity where none was intended, had served that body well many times before. Home Office officials, on the other hand, had much experience in such matters and saw through the prevarication. Government pressure was brought to bear on the Dudley authorities, who responded with a minimum effort to achieve an adequate standard. Thus was a financial disaster for the county police force averted. However, Dudley policemen were still complaining about their accommodation to the chief constable in 1919. In what was termed by the *Express and Star* newspaper as a frank meeting, Walker met with the Dudley policemen and promised to bring what pressure he could upon the Government Inspector, to improve the housing.

The quality of the uniform worn by the Dudley men was never very good. Policemen parading for duty were sometimes obliged to wear poorly fitting uniforms that were threadbare and extensively patched. This became a particular problem during the years of the First World War when uniform issues were reduced. Nevertheless, policemen in other parts of the county were never allowed to let their uniforms deteriorate to such a level.

Successive Inspectors of Constabulary had passed adverse comment upon the quality and costs of the uniform. There appeared to be no obvious benefits to the borough by paying more to have inferior clothing made locally. It was 1914 before the services of a nationally acknowledged uniform supplier were engaged by the borough. Helmets and caps, on the other hand, had no local source. They had to be purchased from a specialist manufacturer. However, in the early part of the twentieth century an opportunity to economise presented itself to the watch committee and was not allowed to escape. A consignment of bush hats was purchased, to be worn instead of the usual helmets and caps. Once again the borough force was set apart from county colleagues, and made to look ridiculous for good measure.

Netherton (Dudley) Section 1907
Wearing the bush hats which replaced the headgear worn by the Dudley police for a short period.
FR: PC Alfred Shilvock, Sergeant William Brunton, Inspector George Burford, PC Henry Haggett
2nd: PC Peter Mobbs, PC Charles Gardiner, PC Richard Phillips
3rd: PC Walter James, PC James Eden, PC Albert Collins

The 'marriage' between the county and the borough continued to be a troubled affair, with the watch committee routinely threatening to destroy the union if it did not get its own way. There had to be a limit to how often the break-up card could be played. That moment arrived early in 1914 when the chief constable proposed to an SJC meeting that the existing agreement with Dudley be terminated. He recommended a fresh arrangement in which the divisions of responsibility were re-drawn in favour of the county. He also suggested that a member of the watch committee should join the SJC. Walker's idea received the full support of the committee members.

Predictably the watch committee was reluctant to have its wings clipped, and devised its own scheme in which the borough gained maximum control of its police force with the minimum financial outlay. A stalemate was reached when the county authorities rejected the Dudley formula.

In 1915 the watch committee cast around for more favourable options and, in doing so, contacted the Clerk to the Staffordshire SJC and asked if police cover could be arranged for the borough. Nothing came of these overtures and, in the same year, the Dudley Watch Committee recommended that "…in future the borough should have its own police and that the watch committee be empowered to arrange accordingly." The recommendation received favourable consideration from the borough council but was put on a back burner until the war was over.

On 3rd February 1920, the Dudley Borough Council met to consider the proposal to create its own borough police force. The watch committee had prepared a report in which the only additional cost foreseen was extra pay for a new chief constable. As a guide, the committee had suggested a further £100 to £150 would be sufficient to cover this. The report did not consider an increase in the police establishment and expected the police to continue as the fire brigade. In the preparation of its report the watch committee acknowledged the proposal by the county to re-draft the agreement between the two authorities, which did not include the fire brigade. The watch committee estimated that a separate fire brigade would cost at least £3,500, perhaps even £4,500, set against the current cost of £1,100. The prospect of a separate fire brigade was too frightening to contemplate.

In January of the same year, Mr Willis Bund, chairman of the Police Authority, had written to the watch committee. He reiterated the county's distaste at the existing situation and pointed out that to enable the police force to remain efficient and to counteract the fire brigade drain on manpower the Dudley division should be increased by eight to ten men immediately. As he wrote his letter Bund must have known there was no possibility of the watch committee agreeing to such a proposal. Indeed, he may have been applying the necessary pressure, ensuring the split between the county and the borough gained momentum. In the event, the final vote was surprisingly close. Thirteen Dudley council members voted against a borough police force whilst sixteen supported the proposal.

The *Police Review* for 12th March 1920, carried an advertisement requesting applications for the post of chief constable of Dudley. Included in his duties would be the captaincy of the fire brigade, and inspector, under the Explosives Acts. His annual salary was fixed at £500. Applicants were required to have previous police experience and be aged between forty and forty-five years.

The watch committee received thirty-six applications for the post, but none were from Worcestershire policemen. Six applicants were selected for interview. They were: Mr A Wright, Chief Constable of Newark on Trent; Mr H P Payne, a Metropolitan Divisional Inspector; Mr J N Campbell, Chief Constable of Bacup; Mr G W Rowbotham, Chief Clerk and Chief Inspector at Oldham; Mr C Smith, a Detective Inspector from Rotherham; Mr H Darley, an Inspector and Chief Clerk in Leeds City.

The interviews were conducted on 24th March 1920, and a tall Scotsman, Mr J N Campbell, was chosen. He was forty years of age and had nineteen years' police experience behind him. As the chief constable of Bacup, a small town twenty-two miles north east of Manchester, he was also the captain of the local fire brigade. He had served at Bacup for six years' having transferred from Clitheroe where he had been chief constable for about a year.

On 1st April 1920, Mr Campbell took up his post as the first chief constable of the Dudley borough police force. He was joined by fifty-two former Worcestershire policemen who had all agreed to remain in the force. Campbell served at Dudley for twenty-six years.

The only officer to return to the county was Superintendent Rudnick, who had acted as caretaker of Dudley police whilst in charge of the Bromsgrove division, following the retirement of Chief Superintendent Richard Speke on 31st October 1919.

Chief Superintendent Richard Speke
Dudley
1893 - 1919

Superintendent Charles Rudnick

Superintendent Charles Rudnick was also one of the men to return to the county from Birmingham in 1911. He was a larger than life character who rarely missed a photo opportunity, but who pursued his duties with tenacity. Rudnick was born in London in 1857 and joined the British Mercantile Marine at the age of fourteen. When he was eighteen he joined the Duke of Cornwall Regiment, serving in Bermuda and Gibraltar.

**Inspector (later Superintendent) Charles Rudnick at Castle Street
with a prisoner believed to be named Whallings.
Whallings was found to be in possession of a revolver
when Rudnick arrested him following a wounding incident
at Leigh Sinton c1910**

Charles Rudnick was a stocky, almost barrel-shaped man who displayed a tattoo of a ship in full sail when he exposed his chest. He joined the force in 1880 when he was twenty-four years old. He married his wife Edith four years later and they had a son and daughter.

Rudnick was a keen sportsman and encouraged his men to take part in a variety of sports, wherever he was stationed in the county. He had previously served at Dudley for three years at the beginning of the twentieth century. During his time there he formed a swimming club and a cricket club and was able to raise funds to equip the cricket team with suitable clothing. He was also directly responsible for the provision of a billiard table and other games equipment in the recreation room at the police station.

Charles Rudnick retired on a pension, at Bromsgrove in 1921, after more than forty years service. He was to continue his interest in the local police sports club until his death in 1932.

Chapter Ten

Memorial to the fallen

October 1920 was a time for the force to remember those colleagues lost in the war. The newly formed Police Federation suggested to the chief constable that a memorial stone should be erected, and it was agreed that the stone should be fixed to the outside wall of the police headquarters in Castle Street, Worcester.

There was no official funding for the war memorial, so the chief constable asked each officer to donate money on a pre-set scale according to rank. The contributions requested were quite substantial, but few wished to be seen showing signs of reluctance for such a cause.

On 28th July 1921, the chairman of the SJC, Mr Bund, unveiled a white stone panel that incorporated the badge of the Worcestershire Constabulary and was inscribed as follows:

> In memory of the men of the Worcestershire Constabulary
> who gave their lives for their Country in the Great War
> 1914 – 18
>
> Percival G Bicknell
> William Bould
> Ernest Bullock
> Cyril Davies
> Ernest Haynes
> Arthur Hemming
> Alfred G Hurren
> Oswald P Pollard
> George Pratt
> Maurice W Saunders
> James Simpson
> Alfred A Stokes
> Albert E Taylor
> John E Taylor
> Joseph W Tromans
>
> Lest we forget

A contingent of policemen and relatives of those lost in the war watched as the ceremony took place.

Industrial unrest

In 1921 the country was heading towards severe financial problems. The county was forced to suspend police recruiting, reduce police pay and curtail uniform issue. This in turn placed considerable pressure on police resources at a time when miners were striking and railwaymen were expected to follow. In the Halesowen district, twelve emergency special constables were sworn in and sixty extra policemen were drafted into the area from other parts of the county.

For the police, the strikes of the 1920s were similar to the industrial unrest of 1910, when miners in South Wales took action in support of a small group of their colleagues who were locked in a wrangle over the rate of pay for a particular coal seam. On 7th November the miners attacked Ton-y-Pandy pit-head and this led to an extended period of rioting and looting. The local police were overwhelmed and called for assistance. A number of forces responded, including Worcestershire who sent twenty men. These men were away from their homes for several months. They communicated with their families by letter and occasionally had group photographs taken of themselves, posing in front of the pit-heads. These pictures were printed onto postcards and sent to friends and relatives at home. The conditions in which they were obliged to live were particularly primitive, but made tolerable by parcels from home containing clean clothes and food.

Life in the valleys proved to be rough, with repeated incidents of violence in which the police were often required to make baton charges whilst being pelted with stones by the miners. Injuries on both sides were frequent. PC Ralph Ballard from Stourbridge was struck by a piece of rock that cut through his helmet, causing a nasty gash to his head. It required five stitches to join the wound.

Returning to 1921, the force borrowed one hundred revolvers and holsters from the Admiralty. Six Halesowen policemen were selected to carry weapons during the emergency, with the bulk of the weapons being held at headquarters. Fortunately, there was never a need to use the firearms in anger, but at least one baton charge was necessary, at Langley on 19th May 1922.

PC Ralph Ballard at the Pen-y-Craig coal pit, South Wales, during the strike in 1911

Whilst police resources continued to absorb a demanding workload, Sinn Feiners were suspected of taking advantage of the disruption by setting fire to hayricks around Birmingham and Kidderminster. The chief constable enthused about a simple device called a 'poacher alarm' and recommended it to local farmers. The alarm comprised a length of wire that was set up around a haystack about a foot (300mm) above the ground. If the wire was touched, it activated a gun. No details were given of the type of gun to be used, its ammunition, or the direction of fire. The contraption was claimed to be effective but there is no record of it ever being successful.

The General Strike of 1926 brought further disruption to the county when selected workers in key industries withdrew their labour. The chief constable instructed his superintendents to keep him informed of all developments. At Halesowen, Superintendent William Lyes reported that electricity-board employees at Smethwick were to be sworn in as special constables to protect electrical establishments at Halesowen and Oldbury. A further one hundred and twenty-four employees of Messrs. Stewart and Lloyd of Coombs Wood Tube works were also to be appointed special constables to guard their works in shifts of twenty-four. Superintendent William Milsom told the chief constable that the trains, buses and trams would cease operations at Oldbury, and a similar situation was described by Superintendent Frederick Smith at Redditch. Superintendent Smith also gave details of a large, open-air meeting held at Church Green West, which was addressed by Mr. F. G. Lloyd, the prospective Labour candidate for the Kidderminster division and a Mr R. L. Lewis of the South Wales Miners Federation. He considered both speeches to be moderate in their tone.

Superintendent William Milsom c1920

In most cases the relationship between the police and the strikers was one of indifference, but occasionally there were outbursts of disorder, particularly when the strikers disapproved of activities designed to thwart their aims. In one example, at Oldbury, Superintendent Milsom was asked by the Fuel Controller in Birmingham to supervise the removal of eight barges containing two hundred tons of fuel-oil, from Clayton's Wharf to the Shell Mex depot. The distance of about a mile required the negotiation of nine locks. Milsom turned up on a Friday evening at about 7.00p.m, with thirty-seven men, only to discover a crowd of about six hundred people had assembled to stop the barges. The superintendent and his men cleared the tow-path and he stationed policemen at intervals along the route. The crowd quickly moved ahead of the convoy of barges in order to immobilise one of the lock gates. The policeman who was in charge of the lock had to draw his staff in a desperate attempt to disperse the crowd. They did move, but not before one of them had been struck by the officer. By 10.00p.m. the work was completed and the barges discharged their loads. Meanwhile the strikers sank a canal boat containing pig iron at the entrance to the depot where the fuel oil had been delivered. This effectively prevented any further barges entering or leaving. The following afternoon Milsom went to Hickens Bridge, Tat Bank, with twenty-seven officers to protect workmen who were attempting to raise the sunken barge. They were greeted by a very hostile crowd of about four hundred men. Once again the policemen were able to clear the area to enable the barge and its load to be recovered and removed to Brades Steel Works.

Police holidays suffered as the chief constable postponed the taking of annual leave. He did allow weekly rest days with some restrictions. Policemen could not leave their districts without their superintendent's permission, and they had to be regularly available for duty after 10.00p.m.

By the end of May 1926 it was assessed that tensions had eased, and policemen were allowed weekly rest days without interference and to catch up on their annual holidays. However, it was some time before the men were permitted to be further than thirty miles from their district when off duty.

Married life for a policeman

Life for policemen was not only tough at work, but domestic arrangements for married men were far from satisfactory. Before the war, approximately half of the married policemen were provided with appropriate quarters. In 1911, in an effort to conserve the housing supply, the chief constable decided that men with less than three years' service would not be allowed to get married. New recruits who were married when they joined were required to live in single accommodation for at least twelve months before being allocated married quarters. Not surprisingly, this decision proved to be a double-edged sword. The housing supply was controlled efficiently, but the force lost many good men who found this particular condition of service quite unacceptable. In 1921 the chief constable relaxed the rules in certain, undefined, cases. The impact of this decision is difficult to assess, but the instruction was set to continue for most police officers, for many more years to come.

Women and the Worcestershire Constabulary

The outbreak of war led to a reassessment, in many quarters, of the role that women could, and should, undertake. A few police forces in England and Wales took advantage of this enlightened thinking, but Worcestershire was not one of them. When the evidence is assessed, there is no doubt that successive chief constables of the county, in the first half of the twentieth century, failed to appreciate, either through naivety or plain arrogance, the role women played within their police force.

The formation of female pressure groups to promote feminine viewpoints led to a series of letters being received by the chief constable from groups such as the Worcestershire Federation of Women's Institutes and the Malvern Society for Equal Citizenship. Each letter urged Walker to appoint female police officers, but their contents cut little ice. In March 1917 he issued an instruction that forbade the wives of police officers seeking work without his sanction, although he made exceptions for those women who were engaged in work of national importance. The wives of those policemen who were in charge of a station with a telephone or cells were ordered not to seek employment.

Walker turned up the pressure on police families in 1922 when he told them that it was the duty of policemen's wives to look after country police stations when their husbands were out. Continuing in the same autocratic tone, he told them that the officer's future prospects could be affected by the failure of his wife to understand her responsibilities.

This outburst followed an incident in which a policeman who was in charge of a country beat had to close his station when he went out, because his wife refused to stay at home and look after it while he was out. Unfortunately, the chief constable felt unable to deal with the matter as the isolated incident that it no doubt was. He gave no credit to the wives of policemen who tirelessly supported their husbands, sometimes in unpleasant circumstances. In one incident, a nasty situation confronted Alice Jeffs and her youngest daughter at Ripple police station, whilst her husband Richard was out. She answered a knock at the back door and was faced with a man who threatened her, and demanded money and food. Fortunately the family terrier dog took a dislike to the intruder and set about him. PC Jeffs returned a few moments later and arrested the man, who it transpired had just been released from Gloucester Gaol. The prisoner had watched the house until the policeman went out and then approached what he had concluded was an easy target.

Ripple police station was located alongside the A38, the main Worcester to Gloucester road, in a fairly isolated position. The lone house must have been a beacon to tramps and vagabonds who frequented the countryside as late as the 1960s and 70s. Alice Jeffs' experience is similar to those encountered by other policemen's wives who had lived in the house. Ivy, the wife of PC Cyril Sanders, endured a number of these unwelcome and persistent callers in the years leading up to the Second World War. Years later she recalled the isolation she felt at those times.

Policewomen

In March 1919 the Home Office wrote to the chief constable to encourage him to employ policewomen. He sought the views of surrounding forces, and by the time he reported the correspondence to the police sub-committee it was a forgone conclusion that policewomen would not be engaged in Worcestershire.

The subject received scant attention over the next few years, in spite of letters sent in by various women's groups and a Home Office letter in 1935. In September 1937 the magistrates at Stourbridge raised the question once again when they asked for policewomen to be employed in the industrial north of the county. Lloyd-Williams, the chief constable at the time, brushed aside the request when he told the SJC that any duties carried out by the women police could be adequately carried out by the male police. Nothing further was done.

The outbreak of the Second World War caused the subject to be revisited in a limited fashion. Uniformed women were taken on across the force to act as clerks, and were known as auxiliary policewomen. They had no police powers and their skills in shorthand and typewriting were considered more important than any other qualities.

In 1944, sixteen women were chosen from the auxiliary staff to serve as patrol policewomen. They received six weeks' initial training at Castle Street, or as one policewoman put it, "...square bashing with Bill Gibson shouting at us." Practical training was provided when they were sent for attachment to the Birmingham and Gloucestershire forces, where there were already fully fledged policewomen employed. The patrol policewomen had the same powers as policemen, but tended to concentrate upon incidents involving sexual offences, children and care matters.

PW Inspector Margaret Jones c1966

When the war ended, the employment of policewomen became a bargaining chip between the Home Office and Lloyd-Williams, who was still opposed to them. He found that an increase in his male establishment could only be achieved by setting up a proper policewomen's department. At the end of November 1945 the Home Office gave its blessing to his application for the force to take on one policewoman sergeant and sixteen policewomen. Five days later the chief constable had appointed the first seven, all former auxiliary policewomen. They included Margaret Jones and Phyllis Calder, both of whom came from police families. They were both destined to lead the policewomen's department through the 50s 60s and 70s.

PW Phyllis Calder
c1948

Telephones

As the telephone system in the county continued to develop, police telephone communications improved as well. All main stations had at least one line, and many of the rural stations were equipped as well. Superintendents made sure that they had a telephone in their offices, in addition to any other that might be in the station. In 1924 the Gloucestershire branch of the National Farmers Union asked the chief constable to install telephones at all stations with married constables. The request was refused. In a decision inconsistent with his earlier observations about policemen's wives, Walker ruled that in the absence of the constable there would be no one to look after the telephone or prevent its improper use. There was also a risk of the station rapidly becoming a public telephone office, and its probable use for police purposes would not justify the expenditure.

Typists and typewriters

On 1st January 1922, Miss Irene Knott of Albany Road, Worcester, was taken on as the force's first typist. She was paid £2.0.0d a week, and when she resigned in 1924 she was replaced by Miss Olga Street, at a lesser salary of £1.15.0d (£1.75). The force headquarters had been using typewriters since 1913 and the employment of a typist was a departure from the routine of policemen as clerks. It was also an early move towards civilianisation, although for many years the force had employed matrons for female prisoners and cooks for the single men. Gradually typewriters began to appear at divisional stations across the force. They were generally second-hand machines costing nine or ten pounds each.

Prisoner transport

On 15th March 1922, HM Prison Worcester finally closed its doors, and all male prisoners were transferred to Winson Green in Birmingham. This created security problems for the police who had to deliver remanded and convicted prisoners over longer distances. At the end of 1925 the question of transporting prisoners to Winson Green from the north of the county was re-opened. The subject had last been on the agenda in 1887, when the provision of suitable transport had been refused. The situation had changed little since that time except that the number of prisoner escorts had increased considerably. There were a variety of arrangements in place depending upon where the prisoners were being taken from. All of them were unsatisfactory. Some of the prisoners and their escorts travelled by rail to Winson Green station, and then had to make their way on foot through a very 'undesirable quarter' where the risk of escape was great. Others were taken to New Street railway station. From there they were led to Edmund Street, where they waited in a queue for a tram to Winson Green. In some cases, where there was no train available, the prisoners were taken on a bus. Not unnaturally, the police were unhappy about the situation, but the members of the public who had to travel on the same public transport as the prisoners protested even louder. Some of the offenders were verminous and totally unsavoury in their hygiene and language. Often their manners and behaviour made their company deeply offensive. Initially, efforts were made to hire transport to and from the prison, but the majority of taxi proprietors would not entertain the idea. Those who did gave exorbitant quotations, which, whilst reflecting their reluctance to provide a service, also added substantially to the annual transport costs of the force whenever their offers were taken up.

By now the Staffordshire and Birmingham police forces had bought purpose-built motor transport to take their prisoners to gaol. The benefits that such vehicles provided were not lost on the Worcestershire chief constable. After much deliberation the police sub-committee was convinced that a prison van was necessary, and a one-ton Morris chassis with a prison van mounted on it was chosen. The cost of the vehicle was £295, with a further £30 spent on a self-starter, fire extinguisher, speedometer and insurance. The van was registered on 26th March 1926, as NP 8087 and was based in the north of the force. When not required to transport prisoners it was used as a personnel carrier for police officers.

On patrol in the 1920s and 30s

The responsibilities of a policeman working nights in the 1920s and 30s were quite different to those of a modern day police officer, particularly in the towns. When the pubs closed and the drunks disappeared from the streets, the night bobby was king of his beat. He would begin to check the shops and other lock-up premises for security. The night shift was the time when the policeman would work eight consecutive hours instead of the split shifts endured by his daytime colleagues. He was expected to check property on his beat, once before and once after his break. The routine would be to try door handles and examine all windows for security. When he found premises that were insecure, the officer would contact the owner or keyholder to inspect the premises with him. If that was not possible, the officer would have his own methods of securing the premises, or at least marking the entrance in such a way that it would be easy to detect whether a person had entered. This might be a piece of paper wedged between the door and the frame, or a wetted strand of hair from his head, stuck across a window and its frame. Some of the methods he used were quite ingenious, fuelled by the fact that it was in the officer's own interest to ensure that there was no crime on his beat. If something occurred and he failed to find it, then the next morning he would be called from his bed to explain why it had happened.

In the daytime, policemen were called upon to deal with a wide range of incidents, but few could be more dangerous than a runaway horse, as new recruit PC George Skerratt found when he distinguished himself at Redditch on 13th July 1927. The incident happened in Hewell Road, where George was patrolling on foot. He saw a horse harnessed to a float come galloping into view, heading for the town centre. The horse was terrified and had already travelled about a quarter of a mile at full speed. Four men stood in the horse's path but were unable to slow it down and there was a near tragedy as the horse almost struck a motor car travelling in the opposite direction. The officer tried to stop the horse by using his cape but this failed. He managed to grab the back of the float as it went past. In a scene more suited to a western movie, he was dragged behind the vehicle before climbing on board. He managed to take hold of the reins and eventually brought the horse and float to a halt. George was not injured and was later specially commended for his conduct.

PC George Skerratt Redditch c1927

Traffic control was a fairly routine activity. On Whit Monday, 27th May 1928, the force was saddened when an extremely popular officer was killed whilst controlling traffic in Malvern. At about 8.45p.m. PC Sidney Overton was helping crowds of people to cross the main road, to and from Malvern Link railway station. The officer was standing in the centre of the road when he caught sight of a two and a half year old boy, running from a drinking fountain to his mother on the other side of the road. As the boy ran in front of a motor car, Sidney stepped forward to push him back and they were both

PC Howard Overton Malvern c1927

struck by the car. The boy received a glancing blow, but the policeman was knocked into the path of a car travelling in the opposite direction. The injuries he received from this collision proved fatal.

The residents of Malvern Link were sufficiently moved by PC Overton's death to ask that the following be read at the inquest: "The residents express their sympathy with Mrs Overton and family on losing one who always did his duty cheerfully and with a smile and was a protector and friend to us all."

Sidney Overton left a widow, Barbara, and a daughter, Marjorie, aged twenty-one. Barbara received a widow's pension of £82.12.3d (£82.61) per annum.

Generally, the death of a husband and father could prove to be catastrophic for the family left behind. Police families faired marginally better with the provision of a pension and allowances for those children under the age of fifteen. Unfortunately, even these payments were often insufficient to keep a family together. Extra help came in the form of the Gurney Fund. The Gurney Fund was founded in 1890 by Catherine Gurney and was financed by donations and regular contributions from most policemen. Miss Gurney established a children's home at Redhill in Surrey for children of police families, including orphans, or the youngsters of a remaining parent who could not look after them. A number of children from county police families benefited from their time at the home, including those of PC Benjamin Round who died at Stourbridge in 1924. He had six children; Benjamin, Edith, Frederick, Samuel, Edna and Olive. Their ages ranged from five to eighteen when he died, and because their mother was unable to support them all the younger ones found a new home at Redhill.

PART IV

Chapter Eleven

New law, fresh demands

>They say that the poor Prime Minister
>Has a day that never ends.
>A-arguing with his enemies
>And fighting with his friends.
>He has forty million worries at least
>You will agree, but
>He hasn't got as many as the poor PC.

This verse was printed in a national newspaper in 1930 and served to illustrate just how much new law had been, and was being, created. It all meant more work for the policeman.

Amongst this legislation was the Road Traffic Act of 1930, which introduced new law as well as drawing together and updating existing traffic law. A consequence was the need for the police to make greater use of motor vehicles to enforce it.

Motor patrol

In December 1930, the police sub-committee approved the purchase of eight Royal Enfield 9.76 h.p. motorcycle combinations. Each machine cost £94.15.0d (£94.75). At the same time two Austin 15.9 h.p. touring cars were bought to enable sergeants to supervise the motorcycle patrols, which would operate from Stourbridge and Worcester.

The new motor patrol assembled at the rear of the police headquarters in Castle Street, Worcester c1931
LtoR: PC Reginald Hemming, PC Stanley Pennington, Deputy Chief Constable Thomas Pennington, PC John Wheeler and PC Edward Williams.

Police officers were invited to apply to join the new 'motor patrol'. They had to be experienced motorcyclists with some mechanical knowledge. Day to day maintenance of the machines would be their responsibility, but for more specialist work the machines went back to the Royal Enfield works at Redditch. The deputy chief constable, Thomas Pennington, interviewed each of the applicants. Amongst the first to be appointed were PC Reginald Hemming, PC Edward Williams, PC John Wheeler and PC Leslie Warner. They were each posted to headquarters in January 1931. Later in the year the Stourbridge motor patrol was set up.

It soon became apparent that communication with, and control of, the patrols was going to be a problem. As soon as they drove out of the station yard they were on their own. After much deliberation it was decided that about twenty beat stations situated on main roads would each have a telephone installed. It then became the responsibility of the patrols to call at these stations to check for messages from headquarters. These unscheduled visits to the rural stations rapidly became extremely unpopular with the resident policemen and their families. A new idea was called for and it was the motor patrol crews who thought of it. They cut a number of lengths of wood, one for each rural police station. The wood was similar to a roofing batten in size and was painted white. Each batten measured about ten inches (24cms) in length and was pointed at one end. It was fixed to a top corner of each police notice board by means of a pre-drilled screw hole close to the opposite end from the point. Each batten was then able to pivot on the screw that secured it to the notice board. Normally the batten pointed down, but if there was a message for the motor patrol then the officer at the station, or his wife, would turn the batten to point skywards. With these unconventional signalling devices it was possible to maintain a rudimentary message-exchanging system between headquarters and the patrols.

Each patrol comprised a constable who rode the motorcycle and an observer who was carried in the sidecar. The vehicle was equipped with a speedometer to enforce speed limits, but initially there was no way of ensuring that it was reading correctly. To deal with this problem the motor patrol officers measured out an exact mile near to Kerswell Green, Kempsey. They used a milestone indicating six miles to Worcester as the first point of reference, and a stake secured in the hedgerow, seventeen feet (5.18 metres) short of the seven miles to Worcester milestone, as the second. The speed of the police motorcycle could now be measured against a stop-watch with absolute certainty.

The motorcyclists did not have to work nights. Normally they would work day shifts, but occasionally they would commence duty at 6.00a.m. and sometimes they would have to work an evening shift. Duty was in segments of two four-hour periods and the motor patrol would cover about seventy to one hundred miles in each period. In addition to their enforcement role, the patrols were used to move police mail around the force as well as collect police circulars, such as the *Police Gazette*, which arrived daily by rail at Shrub Hill railway station.

There was a certain panache to being a police motor-cyclist and the men were proud of their smart uniforms and highly polished machines. Whilst many of their colleagues envied them, not everyone in the force was an enthusiast. As a matter of routine the motor patrol men were expected to call in at divisional police stations to liaise, deliver and collect mail and pick up messages and instructions. At Oldbury, Superintendent Peter Mobbs had no time whatsoever for these men. He thought that they looked like cinema attendants in their outfits and told them so in no uncertain terms whenever he could. His behaviour got to be so bad that the motor patrols would only visit his station when they knew he was out.

Superintendent Peter Mobbs

Peter Mobbs joined the force in 1897, passing the comment that he did not expect to stay above three months. He can be appropriately described as 'one of the old school', finding it difficult to embrace change and progressive ideas. Mobbs served all over the county with a break for army service during the First World War. He was a strict, efficient and fearless man, who, as he rose through the ranks, also gained a reputation because of his bombastic manner. In his pamphlet, *The Young, the Old and the In-Between*, Tom Bainbridge described him as "a solid chunk of a man, with no neck and a square pugnacious face". Amongst his many pet hates were open inkwells. Whenever he came across one he would roar loudly and strike it shut with his cane. He married Louisa Dews of Stirchley in 1900 and they had two children, a daughter Louisa and a son named after the chief constable, Herbert Sutherland. Herbert followed his father into the police force. At the time of his retirement in 1936, Peter Mobbs was described as the father of the county force, but it is not clear who conferred the title upon him.

Inspector (later Superintendent) Peter Mobbs
Oldbury c1928

PC Stanley Hill

As with the maintenance of the motorcycles, the force utilised the skills of its men wherever it could. PC Stanley Hill was such a man. He spent all of his service stationed at Redditch and it was a rare, much prized event to see him patrolling the streets. Stanley was a native of Lye and had previously been a machinist before joining the police in 1921. No doubt his civilian skills led to him being employed as the station handyman, a job that seemed to keep him fully occupied. He also gained the nickname 'tinners' from the standard comment he made when confronted with a repair job, 'a bit o' tin'll do that.' After a chequered career in the police force, Stanley retired and took a job as an ambulance driver. As a result of an accident, he had to leave his ambulance work and, in 1962, took a job as - the Redditch police station handyman.

More boundary changes

On 1st April 1931, Worcestershire's boundaries with Warwickshire and Gloucestershire were re-drawn. Warwickshire took Alderminster, Shipston on Stour, Tidmington and Tredington, whilst Worcestershire added Ipsley and part of Bickmarsh. Gloucestershire got Blockley, Cutsdean, Daylesford, Evenlode, Red Marley d'Abitot, Staunton, Chaceley and Teddington, whilst Worcestershire gained most of Pebworth, Ashton under Hill, Aston Somerville, Childswickham, Cow Honeybourne, Hinton on the Green, Beckford and Kemerton. This all followed a similar agreement in the north of the force in 1928 when part of the Oldbury division was transferred to the Borough of Smethwick. These changes represented very little adjustment in police terms, although at Oldbury a number of officers became available to be deployed in other parts of the county.

The census of 1931 revealed that there was a population of 279,266 in Worcestershire, with an authorised police establishment of 351. This gave an average of one constable to every 795 persons, and placed the county roughly halfway down the list of fifty-eight county forces. Kidderminster was closer to the bottom on a similar list of borough forces. With a strength of thirty-eight officers for a population of 29,521, it made an average of one officer to 777 of the population. This position worsened in April 1933 when the area of the borough was extended and the population estimated at 32,410.

Walker's departure

Early in 1931 the chief constable, Lieutenant Colonel Herbert Sutherland Walker, gave notice that he intended to resign his post on 30th September 1931. He had been the chief constable for more than twenty-eight years. In the latter years of his service he was considered by many to be an old man who had lost control, and allowed his senior officers to rule the roost.

Walker died on 13th April 1932, aged sixty-six. His wife ensured that his memory lived on when she made a financial contribution to the force that enabled the setting up of the Worcestershire Constabulary Benevolent Fund. Subsequently most policemen voluntarily contributed to the fund. In 1964 the Fund had assets of

£19,743.17.1d (£19,743.85) and was supporting seventy-two widows and seven children. It was wound up in 1967.

Captain James Evan Lloyd-Williams

The new chief constable was Captain James Evan Lloyd-Williams. He married Lillian Roche Brett in 1923 and they had two daughters. He took up his post on 1st October 1931, and came from a quite different background to his predecessors. He was born on 7th April 1888, into a family that had produced a number of clergymen in Wales. His father, James Lloyd-Williams, was the headmaster of The Schools at Oswestry.

Captain James Evan Lloyd Williams CBE, MC, DL
Chief Constable of the Worcestershire Constabulary
1931 - 1958

Lloyd-Williams attended St. Peters College, Westminster, until 1907, when he applied to join the Indian Police. Once accepted, he arrived in India on 2nd December 1907, as a probationary assistant superintendent of police. When he had completed his training he served at Gaya, Ranchi, Calcutta, Midnapur, Palamau and Darbhanga in Eastern India. He joined the 35th Scinde Horse in the Derajat Mobile column on the North West Frontier, following the outbreak of the Great War. Later he served in Mesopotamia with he 33rd Light Cavalry and 32nd Lancers. He was awarded the Military Cross for his services at the Battle of Shargat in 1918.

In 1927 Lloyd-Williams became chief constable of Montgomeryshire and held that post until moving to Worcestershire. He was considered more dynamic than his predecessor. This was clearly illustrated by his control of the force and its rapid movement forward to keep pace with the developments of the day. He prided himself in knowing each of his men by name, together with details of their current workload. He also took an interest in their families. When he visited police stations he would ask an officer, "How's the family?", "How is crime?", and, in rural areas, rather unexpectedly, "How are the drains?". Sewage and drains were the source of many complaints from his men. If the policeman was away from the station when he called, Lloyd-Williams would politely deal with the policeman's wife, but would never consider entering the house.

The new chief constable came to be highly regarded, not only by his subordinates but also by many others who came into contact with him. Everything about the man was individual, from his style of walk to his clipped manner of speech. More than ten years after his retirement he was still discussed with affection within the force.

Wage reductions

Lloyd-Williams' arrival coincided with an economic depression that gripped the country. Local and national government were scrutinising expenditure with a view to making savings. Salaries of local government employees were particularly vulnerable. When the National Economy Act was passed, the county council cut the wages of teachers by 10% and policemen by about 5%. Other county employees were not affected but agreed to a reduction of between 2½% and 10%. These reductions were scheduled to last for one year but continued into 1933. The teachers had to wait even longer for their wages to be fully restored. The cuts trimmed a constable's wage by about 5/- (25p) each week.

Police family traditions

On 13th August 1932, Superintendent Gustavus Gray, who was in charge of the Halesowen division, died after a long and painful illness. He was a native of Somerset and had joined the force in 1897. His son, Sidney, and grandson, Robert, followed him into the Worcestershire Constabulary. Superintendent Gray was highly regarded wherever he served, and on one occasion his popularity brought him into conflict with the chief constable. Prior to his promotion to superintendent, he had served as an inspector at Pershore for six years. To express their regret at his departure, a deputation of townspeople, led by a local councillor, went to Halesowen to make him a gift of a clock. When the chief constable got to hear of the presentation he insisted that the clock should be returned, a gesture that no doubt caused the superintendent a great deal of embarrassment.

The Gray family-ties with the police force were not unusual. A number of families became well known because more than one member of the clan had joined the force. There were the Bunns, the Copes, the Gittus', the Males, the Milners, the Mobbs' and the Skerratts, to mention but a few. The Cope family had links in the Herefordshire county force as well. In the comparatively small police community, there are also numerous examples of families becoming linked through marriage.

**Seated: PC Joe Bunn, Deputy Chief Constable Thomas Pennington, PC Percy Bunn
2nd Row: PC Stanley Bunn, PC Walter Bunn, PC James Bunn.
Photo c1930.**

The wind of change

Gustavus Gray was not replaced at Halesowen, but instead the Halesowen division was amalgamated with the Oldbury division under the command of Superintendent Peter Mobbs. Halesowen became a sub-division of Oldbury in the care of Inspector Richard Dainty, who lived at Cakemore. These changes to the policing arrangements did not meet with universal approval. In fact there was considerable resistance from the local justices. The magistrates courts were held on the same day of the week at both Oldbury and Halesowen and it was customary for the local superintendent to prosecute cases before both benches. The new arrangements made that impossible. It took some delicate negotiating by the chief constable to get both benches to change their court days, thereby heading off a major quarrel.

Superintendent Gustavus Gray
Halesowen c1926

Change was not limited to Halesowen and Oldbury; headquarters became known as the headquarters division and was divided into two branches: administration and crime.

Lloyd-Williams introduced new systems to record crime, lost and found property as well as beat incidents, commonly known as 'general occurrences'. He gained approval for another thirty-one police stations to have telephones installed, and by 1936 had arranged for many beat stations to have a telephone extension fitted in the main bedroom, to enable a faster response to emergency calls at night. He also took a more common-sense approach to the use of telephones for private calls by merely insisting that they were paid for.

When he discovered that the motorcyclists on motor patrol were having an inordinte amount of time off duty with sickness, he concluded that this was due to the rugged nature of their work, and replaced the motorcycle combinations with three Hillman Minx cars and one B.S.A. tricar. The two Austin motor cars purchased at about the same time as the motorcycles were replaced with two Wolsley Hornets. The prison van, used in the north of the county, was sold and the job of conveying prisoners fell to the motor patrol crews.

The chief constable continued to develop the motor patrol department, gradually increasing the numbers of men and vehicles over the next few years. By 1938 the crews were required to attend driver training courses at Preston in Lancashire. In 1939, eight new Wolsley 18hp motor cars were delivered by John Bryant of Bromsgrove. As an experiment two of these cars were equipped with loud hailers. All patrol cars by this time had been fitted with 'police' signs.

On 9th September 1933, Lloyd-Williams presented a report to the police sub-committee, in which he proposed setting up a fingerprint and photographic bureau at headquarters. The sub-committee granted £150 for the purchase of equipment and the construction of a darkroom. Sergeant Sidney Inight and DC Thomas Williams were selected to work in the new department. They were sent on a course to the West Riding Police headquarters at Wakefield in October 1933 and received instruction in photography, fingerprint classification and modus operandi.

Sidney William Inight
Assistant Chief Constable
1952 - 1955
Photo c1952

In 1934, for the first time the force began sending its recruits to Wakefield for a twelve-week initial training course. Although the in-house training had been dramatically improved about thirty years before, the new courses ensured that training was uniform and to a national standard. There was a charge of £5 per man, plus food and accommodation. Wakefield soon found that it could not accommodate all potential students, and by the end of 1935 the Birmingham training school began to take some Worcestershire recruits. The chief constable also decided that detectives could be employed in a far more useful role than had previously been the case. Most plain-clothes officers were used to serve summonses and court documents and were not actively involved in the investigation of crime. He sent twelve officers on a detective training course at the Victoria Law Courts in Birmingham. At the conclusion of the course, half of the men obtained more than 75% in the final examination.

More heroic work

The years 1932 and 1933 saw numerous brave rescues by police officers. PC Bennet Greet saved a six and a half year old boy from drowning in the River Severn basin in Stourport. The officer jumped into the water whilst he was fully clothed, swam about twenty-five or thirty feet and brought the boy to the side. He administered artificial respiration until the boy recovered consciousness.

PC Eli Smith rescued a boy from an electric pylon at Newnham Bridge. PC Smith was later presented with the Kings Police medal by HM King George V at Buckingham Palace.

PC William Middleton rescued John Horton from a canal at Oldbury – then arrested him for indecent exposure.

PC William Middleton Oldbury c1928

PC Eli Smith c1920

Dr Oliver Terry F.R.C.P.

In 1935 Dr Oliver Terry of Worcester, who later became the police surgeon for the Worcestershire and West Mercia Constabularies, examined his first recruit for the force. Dr Terry was a native of Pudsey in Yorkshire and for many years was a consultant physician at the Worcester Royal Infirmary. Many police candidates of both sexes have stood in all their glory in Dr Terry's first-floor surgery, clutching their early-morning samples. As they Ooh, Aaah'd and coughed, double-decker buses passed close to the building. Passengers on the top deck must surely have had more than their fare's worth if they chanced to gaze in.

Dr Terry retired from general practice in 1970, and as police surgeon in 1982.

The Second World War

On 29th September 1938, Neville Chamberlain, the British Prime Minister, met with other European leaders in Munich and drew up an agreement with the German Chancellor, Adolf Hitler. It guaranteed 'peace in our time'. On the surface there was a collective sigh of relief, but Hitler's demands for 'Lebensraum', or greater living space for the German nation, in a speech in 1937, had ensured that the British government was not completely taken in by his assurances. As early as 1936 there had been preparations for anti-gas training, and in 1937 the Home Office had circulated to chief constables the details of the recruiting and organising of air-raid wardens who would be their responsibility in their respective areas.

At the beginning of 1938 the county police bought quantities of blankets and 'Union' anti-gas cloth for gas proofing certain designated rooms at police stations. At the same time, wooden shutters were fitted to reduce the danger from bomb splinters.

In 1939 a number of police officers were appointed to carry out air raid precautions (ARP) duties. The strength of the force was increased to allow one inspector, eight sergeants and four constables to be released for ARP work. Meanwhile, police communications were improved and secured when a system of private telephone lines was installed between headquarters and divisional stations.

**Rifle practice at Halesowen at the beginning of the Second World War.
L-R: PC Verly Lancelot, PC William Dancock and PWR Tom Hingley**

In March 1939 the county council appointed an Air Raid Emergency Committee. The controller was the chief constable who was joined by Sir Richard Brooke Bart., Mr H Tomkinson and Mr A C T Woodward. The committee met for the first time on 2nd September 1939.

The outbreak of war signalled a greater use of special constables. About one thousand 'specials' were recruited and equipped with armlets, truncheons and whistles. Five hundred electric hand-lamps were purchased for the specials, and those who were available to perform full-time duties were provided with a complete uniform. The majority of specials took their duties extremely seriously. During an exercise at Alvechurch, Special Constable Albert Ashmore was posted to a bridge, with instructions that no one should cross it. When members of his own family tried to make their way over the bridge he insisted that they turn back, and they did.

As the year 1940 dawned, the government brought home the affects of the war to the population by imposing rationing on sugar, butter and bacon. This was the period commonly termed the 'phoney war'. Although it was the start of the belt tightening, there was little to show that the country was at war. The arrival of petrol rationing added to the pressures, and many motorists mothballed their vehicles for the duration of the war. Those who were able to keep driving found movement at night could be difficult; with no street lighting, their vehicles emitted a thin beam of light, making the roads hazardous to motorists and pedestrians alike. In the vain hope that it may aid safety, the extremities of motor vehicles were painted white.

The first Worcestershire police casualty of the war was reported to the police sub-committee by the chief constable on 25th May 1940. He was Arthur William Cornelius, who died in the Netherlands on 13th May 1940. He was twenty-five years old and came from Swansea.

At the time of the Dunkirk evacuation, fears rose that an invasion by the German Army was imminent. This also gave rise to the possibility of fifth column activities if pro-German, British collaborators, were employed by the Third Reich to prepare the way. As a consequence, Lloyd-Williams was ordered, via secret correspondence from the Home Office, to appoint experienced detectives to work solely on security matters. He chose Detective Sergeant Charles Saull, Detective Constable Colin Cook and Police War Reserve Guy Nevinson. Saull and Cook were given the acting rank of detective inspector and detective sergeant respectively. Other officers were later appointed to similar roles until most divisions were represented. These men were the nucleus of the force's special branch.

PC (later Superintendent) Charles Saull Oldbury c1928

Bombing took its toll on Worcestershire residents, resulting in nineteen deaths and one hundred and thirty injuries by the end of the war. All told, there were 8,864 bombs dropped in the county. One, an oil bomb, dropped at the side of Newtown Road police station in Malvern. It caused superficial damage, but scattered oil everywhere. After the war, when excavations took place to build an office adjoining the house, fragments of the bomb were discovered still embedded in the ground.

Whenever and wherever bombs dropped, the police had to attend the site to collect as much information as they could about the bomb and the damage caused. The crater would be carefully measured to try and establish the capacity of the bomb, and a description of the effect it had had upon the surroundings was recorded. In one such incident on 9th January 1941, three high-explosive bombs dropped at Bricklehampton Hall farm near Pershore, but two of them did not explode. PC Norman Baylis went along to obtain details, and as he approached a number of chicken pens where the bombs lay, they exploded and a cloud of feathers and soil formed in the sky before showering down all over him. The official report states that five portable fowl houses were extensively damaged, half an acre of cabbage destroyed and one hundred fowl killed. At Eldersfield, on 2nd January 1941, two high-explosive bombs dropped, injuring a lamb, which had to be destroyed. The nearby Longdon police station suffered minor damage from the same explosions as plaster fell in one of the bedrooms.

One of the wartime duties for the police was to provide an early warning of air raids. Most police stations had a siren mounted on the roof or a similar, prominent location. The Home Office decided that there should be another method of conveying important messages to the public, so in November 1940, a further five patrol cars were fitted with loudspeakers.

When Coventry was bombed heavily in the same month, Worcestershire policemen were called from their beds at 2.00am and one inspector, two sergeants and twenty-five constables were dispatched to assist their colleagues in the beleaguered city. They were away from home for up to three weeks. A small sacrifice, perhaps, in the scheme of things. Relief contingents continued to be sent to provide assistance and support until the end of the year.

In February 1941 the installation of a regional wireless transmitter was the first movement towards radio communication in the county. Patrol cars and main police stations were fitted with wireless receivers. Detective Superintendent Sidney Inight was given the job of overseeing the wireless project. He had a particular interest in the work, having gained experience in radio communications during the First World War. As the project progressed, a radio transmitter was installed at headquarters, and transmitters as well as receivers were fitted to police cars placed across the force. Although the transmitters in the cars had a range of about ten miles, as receiving stations were based at every major police station, contact with the cars could be maintained with headquarters by land line.

After the war there were further developments as Home Office radio engineers carried out a series of tests to establish the best location for a new VHF aerial for the county and city police. Tests from the Worcestershire Beacon at Malvern revealed that coverage was extremely poor beyond the Clent Hills and around Tenbury. A site at the regional wireless station at Romsley was finally selected, giving a better overall reception, except for a short stretch of road near Malvern.

Lloyd-Williams soon realised that with patrol cars being controlled by wireless, a central point was needed to co-ordinate their work. In 1948 he set up a radio room at headquarters. It was manned twenty-four hours a day and became known as the 'Information Room'.

Worcestershire Constabulary Operations Room at Hindlip Hall c1950
The police officer is unknown

Although the police needed to remain mobile during the war, the chief constable found it extremely difficult to keep the police cars on the road. Even purchasing second-hand vehicles was only partially successful. General repairs and accidents led to problems obtaining replacement parts, and when one Wolsley patrol car was extensively damaged in an accident a similar body shell could not be found. After a search, the body shell of a shooting brake was obtained and mounted on the chassis, transforming the Wolsley's appearance completely.

A national scheme operated by the Ministry of Supply also helped keep police vehicles going. Motor vehicles that were broken down and not repairable were obtained by the Ministry and stripped of their reusable parts. These parts were then recycled to maintain essential vehicles.

In April 1943 a soldier named Stanley Field was granted home leave from the army to help his mother on her small holding. Field was twenty-two years old and had learning difficulties. He had been called up less than twelve months before and was unhappy in the services. Field was due to return to his unit the following month, but failed to turn up. PC Norman Baylis, now of Hartlebury, went to see the young man and advised him to return. During the conversation Field ran away. He had a shotgun with him and fired it in the direction of Baylis but missed. A short while later PC Baylis returned with three colleagues. Field refused to give himself up and fired nine shots at the policemen, but no one was injured. The following day, Thursday 13th May, a larger operation to arrest Field was organised, when twenty-five policemen and ten soldiers moved into the area to search for him. They found him hiding in a cabbage field. He was still armed and determined not to be taken. As the party spread out to encircle the soldier he fired eight times at a range of about forty yards. Two of the policemen were wounded. PC Cyril Webb received pellet wounds to his right arm, in the face and across his body. Sergeant Charles Masters was also caught in the hail of pellets. Although he was seriously hurt, Webb managed to overpower and arrest Field, who was later sentenced to five years' penal servitude at Shrewsbury Assizes.

**PC Norman Baylis with Police Dog Pedro
Mayfields, Redditch c1957**

Cyril Webb's facial injuries resulted in the loss of his right eye. His bravery was acknowledged locally when he received £25 from the SJC. He was later presented with the Kings Police Medal for gallantry.

PC Cyril Webb, his wife Dorothy and their five year old daughter Janet photographed outside Buckingham Palace in February, 1944. Cyril had just been awarded the Kings Police Medal for Gallantry.

He continued to serve in the force, eventually being appointed detective inspector. He was an enthusiastic photographer and for a time was in the Scenes of Crime Department based at headquarters. He retired on a pension on 30th April 1958 and took up a post as assistant superintendent of police in Uganda. Sadly, before the end of that year he died in a motor car accident.

The bravery of other officers involved in the incident was also recognised. PC Frederick Owen, PC Walter Homer and Police War Reserve George Ford each received £5 from the SJC. Sergeant Masters also received £5 from the SJC, and was specially commended and awarded a merit badge.

This was obviously a traumatic incident for all concerned. In such situations the subsequent physical reactions of the individuals involved can vary considerably. At that time it was not the done thing to show any signs of mental anguish, and the effect the incident had upon Sergeant Masters is difficult to gauge. He was medically retired fourteen months later and his failing health was attributed to another distressing occurrence, when he had to deal with the remains of a crashed aircrew at Droitwich mortuary. The police surgeon did not agree that his deteriorating health was anything to do with the consequences of dealing with the crashed aircrew, thus he was not allowed a special pension. Sergeant Masters joined the force in 1919 and fortunately was at the end of the statutory period of service, thereby enabling him to receive a normal pension. He had served in the Royal Army Medical Corps during the Great War. Having been shot by a criminal, then to deal with death in one of its worst settings, coupled with his harrowing experiences of the Great War, this was surely a heavy burden for one person to cope with, particularly when stress was not widely recognised and attracted little sympathy.

Sergeant Charles Masters Oldbury 1936

Cyril Webb was not the only policeman to receive the Kings Police Medal for bravery during the war. Sergeant Alfred Blower received the award after he rescued twenty-five-year-old Leslie Parsons from the River Severn at Stourport on 25th March 1940, during blackout conditions. It was a dark, cold evening and the Severn was in flood when Sergeant Blower heard that the man had fallen into the river. He was able to use his torch to locate Parsons and dived in. Parsons was unconscious when Sergeant Blower got him to the bank, and only recovered after the sergeant administered artificial respiration.

PC (later Sergeant) Alfred Blower Halesowen c1928

Disabled police officers

At least three other policemen who, like Cyril Webb, were disabled, stayed on in the force. PC Frank Peters lost a leg whilst serving in France during the First World War. He was discharged from the Army in 1919 and re-appointed as a constable at Oldbury, where he completed his service as the office reserve. Another Oldbury

PC Frank Peters
Oldbury
c1928

policeman PC Thomas Ward returned from the war in 1919 suffering from 'chronic rheumatism'. He was appointed Superintendent Milsom's orderly, and found station duties to keep him occupied until he retired in 1930. Sergeant Arthur Quarrell also served as a soldier in the First World War. He was wounded in his right eye. The injury caused his eye to deteriorate to the point where it was necessary to remove it and fit an artificial one.

A courageous bobby

Wisdom Stevens was a caravan dweller who set up temporary camp in a field at Blind House Farm, Wythall, in October 1944. As was his wont, it was not long before he went out thieving. PC George Webb soon got to hear that Wisdom had stolen two motor car axles and four motor car wheels, and met the gipsy driving his lorry in Alcester Road. The officer tried to arrest Wisdom, who had other ideas and put the vehicle in reverse. Webb jumped on the running board, and as he was driven backwards at extremely high speed he clung to the vehicle. To try and shake the policeman from the lorry, Wisdom swerved left and right, eventually leaping from the cab as the vehicle careered on. PC Webb was just as quick and leaped from the moving vehicle, grabbing and arresting Wisdom as he did so. This impressive feat earned PC Webb a merit badge and a £5 reward.

The murder of Florrie Porter

On Friday 27th October 1944, at about 8.00a.m., two young schoolboys, Lewis Price and Albert Egan, aged ten and thirteen respectively, arrived at Lickey End School. They saw a woman lying under a glass-covered veranda at the rear of the building. It was the body of thirty-three-year-old Florence Porter of Little Heath Lane, Lickey End. She had suffered stab wounds to the chest and neck and had been beaten about the head. Superintendent James Price and Sergeant John Bryan, from Bromsgrove, were amongst the first officers at the scene, which was later visited by the distinguished forensic scientist Professor James Webster, director of the West Midlands Forensic Science Laboratory.

Professor James Webster c1950

Florrie, as she was known, had lived at home with her mother, two sisters and brother. Her father had died some time before.

Within a short time, her handbag was found close to Norton Farm and her purse near to Townsend Farm. Both farms were situated about half a mile from the murder scene. As part of their search for the murder weapon (a knife) the police drained the nearby Townsend Pool with the help of the fire brigade. They had no success and the weapon was never found.

Police enquiries revealed that Florrie spent a good deal of her spare time in the company of American soldiers. On the evening before the discovery of her body, she was seen drinking in a pub in Bromsgrove with an American army officer who may have been seen later walking her home.

The involvement of an American aroused the interest of the U.S. forces stationed in the area, and there were newspaper reports of 'G' men taking part in the investigations. Certainly the American military police helped with the enquiries and obtained many statements from U.S. servicemen. Police attention focussed on the 123rd (US) Station Hospital in All Saints Road, Bromsgrove. It was a place where a large number of American army officers had been treated before moving on. Numerous identification parades were held and the enquiries, which were supervised by the chief constable, extended all over the country and into France. The ferocity of the attack was such that a question arose over the sanity of the assailant. This led to investigations in the United States to try and identify similar attacks, but without success.

Although there had been a lot of hard, investigative work put in by the police, by the time the inquest was heard on 4th December 1944, the murderer had not been found. The American officer who was said to have accompanied Florrie before her death had not been traced and was known only as Hal.

Police enquiries had quickly identified a suspect named Hal. He was a second lieutenant in the infantry. His full name was Albert J. Lewicke and he was sometimes known as Lewis. During his interview, he admitted knowing Florrie as Flo, but said he had not seen her on the night of her death. Most of his movements were confirmed by his fellow officers and a lady in Redditch whom he had telephoned at about the time of the murder. There were, however, times during that evening and night when his whereabouts were unaccounted for. Unfortunately the evidence amassed against Lewicke was not sufficient to take matters further, coupled with the fact that he was one of thirty Hals residing at the hospital at the time of the murder.

The lack of police success gave rise to a local rumour that the police knew who the offender was, but did not name him for fear of causing a rift in Anglo-American relations at such a crucial time in the war. Although there is no evidence to support the rumour, it persisted for many years.

Sadly, the murderer was never found. Nevertheless, small pieces of information were still being received by the police some fifteen years later.

The Bella mystery

The death of Florrie Porter was not the only murder that required the assistance of Professor Webster during the war. On Monday 19th April 1943, four teenage boys from Lye went to Hagley Wood, just off the main Kidderminster to Birmingham road, near to Hayley Green. They were trying to supplement their wartime rations with a bit of poaching. Whilst in the woods they looked inside a hollow hazel tree, which later became known as the 'Wych Elm'. The tree had a short trunk with wispy branches growing out of its perimeter at the top and from the sides. Inside the trunk it was dark, but the boys were able to make out a human skull, which one of them hooked out with a piece of wood. The youths were concerned that their reason for visiting Hagley Wood was likely to cause them more trouble than reporting what they had found, and so they agreed not to mention the skull. The agreement didn't last long, when one of them told his father. The police were informed and Sergeant Richard Skerratt from Clent police station went to the scene the next day. An examination of the tree and surrounding area by Professor Webster revealed an incomplete skeleton, together with some partial items of clothing. The right shin bone, a 'U' shaped bone from the neck, a kneecap, and some small bones from the hands and feet were missing from the remains.

The remains and the clothing were taken for examination to the Forensic Science Laboratory in Birmingham, where it was established that the skeleton was that of a woman aged around thirty-five years. She was quite short at between 4' 9½" (144cms) and 4' 10½" (146cms), but would have been about 5' 0" (150cms) when wearing the blue, size 5½ Gibson shoes found near the tree. It was estimated that the subject had been dead for between eighteen months and three years, although eighteen months was favoured. The cause of death was likely to have been asphyxiation when part of the female's clothing was forced into her mouth. In later years, one of the youths who found the skull expressed the view that he had forced the material into the base of the skull as he prodded inside the trunk with the piece of wood. This possibility was discounted by Professor Webster during his initial examination.

From Fruit Trees to Furnaces - A History of the Worcestershire Constabulary   133

**PC (later Inspector) Richard Skerratt commences patrol
in Victoria Avenue, Evesham c1936**

Armed with this limited information the police commenced their enquiries under the direction of Detective Superintendent Sidney Inight. Several avenues were pursued at once. Missing persons lists were checked for women of a similar age. There had been a gipsy encampment in Hagley Wood Lane, near to the Wych Elm., Extensive enquiries were made to establish if a gipsy woman had gone missing, but without success. This line of enquiry was further complicated by two letters written to the police by two apparently distraught soldiers, and a further letter written by an Army padre on behalf of another soldier. The letters each related to a gipsy woman named Mary Lee and suggested that she was at risk and likely to commit suicide. In reality each of the letters had been originated by one soldier who had, at the beginning of the war, formed an association with Mary Lee, but had lost contact with her. He hoped that the police would trace her for him so that he could rekindle their affair. A lot of police time was wasted tracing Mary Lee, alias Wenman, alias Beaver, who turned out to be quite safe and in another relationship.

There was more encouraging news on the shoe front. Detective Inspector Thomas Williams visited Leicester and established that the relevant batch of shoes had been manufactured by Clarence Bray Limited of Silesby, between April and June 1940. They had been supplied to two retailers, a mail order company and a footwear wholesaler. Enquiries at these outlets looked very promising initially, but eventually petered out to nothing. In fact, the police had followed up every possible lead, but none had produced any useful information to help identify the dead woman, or establish a motive for her murder.

The whole affair attracted a great deal of press attention. The publicity gave members of the public ample opportunity to exercise their minds concerning the background to the incident. One of the most prominent views was that the murder was part of a witchcraft ritual or a black-magic slaying. This opinion was given more credence by a rumour, which circulated rapidly, that one of the dead woman's hands had been severed and buried elsewhere, apparently the hallmark of witchcraft rites.

Mysterious writings began to appear at various locations in the West Midlands. The first appeared in March 1944 at Upper Dean Street, Birmingham. Scrawled on a brick wall was, "Who put Bella down the Wych Elm – Hagley Wood". Later, other messages appeared in a similar vein. Bella, it transpired, was a witchcraft or black-magic term. The writer or writers of these remarks were never traced.

There was a more down-to-earth answer concerning the missing hand, which, incidentally, was not referred to as such in Professor Webster's report. Several bones of the skeleton had been removed from the tree, not just the small bones from the hands. A search in the vicinity had recovered most of them; in all likelihood they had probably been carried away by animals.

Whilst the murder enquiry was never closed, the opportunity to investigate new information dwindled to nothing and police activities eventually ceased.

More than ten years later a journalist with the *Express and Star* newspaper, Lieutenant Colonel Wilfred Byford-Jones, who wrote under the nom-de-plume 'Quaestor', received a letter that opened up the enquiry once more, and drew the detectives in a new direction. The author of the letter signed herself 'Anna (Claverley)'. She dismissed the witchcraft theory completely and described the victim as a Dutch national who had entered the country illegally in 1941.

Anna was eventually traced and senior police officers interviewed her. Her real name was Una and she had married her former husband, Jack Mossop, in 1932. She had subsequently left Mossop and later settled with her new husband near Claverley in Shropshire. She described to the detectives how, in 1938, Jack started work at the Armstrong Siddeley factory in Coventry, but quickly moved to the Standard Aero works, also at Coventry. In 1940 Jack struck up a friendship with a Dutchman named Van-Ralt. Van-Ralt began to visit the Mossop's home at Kenilworth. Although he always carried plenty of money Van-Ralt did not appear to have a job. Una noticed that whenever her husband and Van-Ralt had been together, Jack always had plenty of money as well. She concluded that the Dutchman was a spy, and she suspected that her husband was passing secrets to him.

In March or April of 1941, Jack Mossop arrived home one evening in a very agitated state and the worse for drink. He told Una that he had been to the Lyttleton Arms, which is a public house at Hagley, with Van-Ralt and a Dutch woman. The Dutch man and woman began to argue, and after a while they all left the pub in a motor car driven by Mossop. After a short distance, Mossop saw the woman slump forward in the front passenger seat as if she had passed out. The Dutchman directed Mossop to drive to a nearby wood where they pushed the woman into a hollow tree. A few months later Una left Mossop, but they did meet occasionally. At one meeting, Jack Mossop told his wife that he thought he was losing his mind because he kept seeing the face of the woman in the tree leering at him. Mossop died in a mental institution in August 1942.

Armed with this new information the detectives once again set about trying to identify the deceased woman. There is no clue in the police records, to establish the conclusion of these enquiries, but, during a television interview in 1958, Professor Webster insisted that the police had identified the murdered woman. If they did, why are the papers not with the file? Certainly, no one seems to have been charged with the offence. Perhaps wartime secrecy means the whole story will never be known.

Counting the cost of war

Eighty-one men from the Worcestershire Constabulary joined the army, whilst fourteen went into the Royal Air Force. Seven men served in the Royal Navy and two in the Royal Marines. Thirteen received commissions in the army and four in the RAF. Four ex-members of the force served with distinction and received the Military Cross, Distinguished Flying Cross, Distinguished Conduct Medal and Distinguished Flying Medal.

Five former policemen were killed during the war. They were: Arthur Cornelius, Oliver Keen, Benjamin Raybould, Samuel Rollinson and Ernest Thomas. A further eight men were wounded and one had to be discharged as medically unfit due to active service.

The end of the war marked an opportunity for the force to undertake a substantial recruiting drive. There was a lot of ground to be made up and there appeared to be a wealth of potential police officers being released from the services. Recruiting was resumed at the end of 1945 and, soon, batches of a dozen or more were being taken on. Indeed, within the next five years, three hundred new recruits joined, but 48% failed to stay the course. Some lasted only a week, whilst others were subsequently weeded out as being unlikely to become efficient police officers. This heavy turnover continued into the 1950s, gradually easing until the losses became more manageable.

PC Gilbert Cook
Kidderminster 1958

The men who joined at this time, and stayed, did not know it but they were the last of the old school and, to some degree, the founders of the new. A number of them became the characters of the force, including eccentrics such as motor patrol officer PC Gilbert Cook, a steam enthusiast who could not resist reciting poetry to transgressing motorists.

On Monday 28th May 1951 a ceremony took place at the new police headquarters, Hindlip Hall, when a memorial plaque was unveiled by the chairman of the Standing Joint Committee, Sir Chad Woodward. The plaque contains the names of those former policemen lost in both wars.

PART V

Chapter Twelve

Kidderminster

The last bastion of police independence in the county, outside Worcester, was the Kidderminster borough force. It had an individuality that its members, and the watch committee administering it, fiercely guarded. This idiosyncratic approach showed in the force's reluctance to harness modern ideas, developments and changes. This was in sharp contrast to the minor revolution being instituted by Lloyd-Williams in the county force.

Officers continued to submit reports to the chief constable, requesting permission to leave the borough whilst off duty. Approval was invariably given, but with the proviso 'if convenient'. Discipline was more severe in the borough, with relatively minor actions or omissions by the officers resulting in an appearance before the chief constable. Whilst the punishments imposed generally had a measure of common sense applied to them, there is a question mark over the discretion allowed to the supervisory officers who were reporting the misdemeanours.

Harry Hodgkinson
Last Chief Constable of Kidderminster Borough Police
1933 - 1947

Opportunities for advancement were not good; in fact deaths and retirements of supervisory officers were generally the only occasions when promotions were possible. Even recruiting was restricted until vacancies were created by promotion or other movement.

The Kidderminster police were also responsible for the ambulance service. This often led to the men being called to incidents outside the borough - at Bewdley, Stourport and the rural parts of Kidderminster. In 1938 the service was called upon 114 times, regularly draining the limited resources available.

For the financial year ending in March 1938, the operating costs for the borough police amounted to £15,240.0.0d, of which the Home Office funded more than half.

The Police Act of 1946 signalled the demise of many borough police forces, of which Kidderminster was one. Since 1840 the county force had made a number of attempts to bring the borough under its wing. Each time, its overtures had been rebuffed. Now, however, legislation required the Kidderminster police force to join its county neighbours on 1st April 1947.

The last of the borough's eleven chief constables, Harry Hodgkinson, retired at the end of March 1947. He had served for more than thirty-nine years. Twenty-five borough policemen transferred into the county force and were permitted to prefix their collar numbers with the letter 'K'.

As the *Kidderminster Times* mourned the passing of the borough police, Captain Lloyd-Williams welcomed the new men to the county, saying, "I am not a slave driver, but I expect good work and I am sure I will get it."

On 9th December 1952, an investigation into the death of PC Franklin Davis commenced. On the previous evening he had paraded for night duty as usual, and was directed to a beat in Kidderminster town centre. The following morning, at the end of his shift, he didn't return to the police station. His colleagues organised a search, in which his helmet was seen floating in the canal lock off Mill Street. When the lock was drained his body was found at the bottom, still clutching his truncheon. A satisfactory reason for his death has never been established.

PC Franklin Davies
Kidderminster Borough Police
March 1947

On 21st March 1953, a Kidderminster man who was facing a court appearance for sending indecent telephone messages decided to end it all, and planned to take his wife with him. He waited until she had gone to bed and then turned on all the gas taps in the house. The smell of the gas woke her up and she tried to get out of the house. Although her husband beat her severely to prevent her leaving, she managed to alert a neighbour, Frank Robinson. He rushed to the borough police box in nearby Mill Street, where he found PC Daniel Nash. It was about 1.30a.m. and the officer was having his meal break in the police box. Both men returned to the house and discovered that it was locked, so the policeman forced an entry. He found that the man had broken the gas pipe in the cellar of the house and was lying unconscious on a heap of coal. Although both Mr Robinson and PC Nash were badly affected by the gas, they were able to get the man out of the cellar and into fresh air, thus saving his life. They were both awarded £10 by the SJC. At a subsequent court hearing, as a result of the man's mental condition, he was sent to Broadmoor.

The Home Secretary, Major G. Lloyd-George, visited Kidderminster on 30th April 1955, to officially open the new police station. The old borough police station in Vicar Street had been operational since the latter part of the nineteenth century. For a number of years it had not been suitable in size or standard of accommodation. An eight-acre site was purchased at Blakebrook, and the new building and twenty-four police houses were constructed by A. H. Guest, for the sum of £166,000.

Bad weather, good work

The beginning of 1947 was outstanding, as it was one of the worst winters in living memory. For about two months the county froze. The complete isolation of some communities was just one of the consequences of the big freeze. Romsley and

From Fruit Trees to Furnaces - A History of the Worcestershire Constabulary   139

Sergeant Basil Sanders c1950

PC Cyril Sanders at Ripple c1940

Hunnington were two of the villages cut off by snow, and PC Basil Sanders, the local policeman, earned a special commendation from the chief constable when he organised the delivery of food supplies to the villagers.

When the thaw came, so did the floods. Low-lying towns and villages, particularly those alongside the River Severn, were quickly under water. Once again the police were on hand to help. Inspector John Heath at Bewdley, Inspector Harold Pitt at Upton upon Severn, PC George Benbow of Severn Stoke and PC Cyril Sanders of Ripple were each specially commended by the chief constable for their outstanding work in the evacuation of victims of the floods.

A dangerous domestic

On 4th May 1948, PC Reginald Lowe was another officer who received a special commendation from the chief constable, but on this occasion it was for courageous conduct. It related to a family dispute he had attended at Newnham Bridge. When he arrived, PC Lowe was confronted by Joseph Pritchard, who was extremely drunk and armed with a .22 rifle. Pritchard had already attacked his father and left him badly injured, and was now threatening to kill him. The officer bravely disarmed the man without further injury to anyone. The SJC rewarded PC Lowe with a cash payment of £10, and he later received the Kings Commendation for Brave Conduct.

Hindlip Hall

In 1946 the county council purchased Hindlip Hall near Fernhill Heath, and a tract of land surrounding it. The hall was earmarked as the new police headquarters, and the SJC allocated more than £61,000 to finance the move and to fund the building of twenty police houses on the site.

The current Hindlip Hall was built in the nineteenth century. An earlier building on the site, known as Hindlip Manor House, dated back several hundred years and was instrumental in hiding fugitives being hunted in connection with the Gunpowder Plot. During the Second World War the hall was occupied by the Royal

Air Force, and a number of wooden huts sprang up around the building to accommodate service personnel. Some of these temporary buildings were retained and utilised by the police, whilst others were removed to a piece of land in Sansome Walk, Worcester, to accommodate the county vehicle registration office.

The move from Castle Street to Hindlip Hall was completed on Sunday 14th September 1947. Although single policemen still remained in quarters at the old building in Castle Street for a little while, the major part of the premises was handed over to the county education department.

A keen sense of humour

The police service has a wealth of folklore. Tales of the escapades of colleagues, some of them long gone, are told, re-told and embellished. Many of the stories only make sense to those in 'the job', because of the shared experience or knowledge that the anecdote requires. Others are just amusing stories. What it does show is that members of the police force are able to laugh at themselves and the situations they find themselves in. In some cases jokes may be considered 'black humour', but nevertheless there is a common understanding of the unsavoury or distressing side of policing that they so often reflect. Many of these yarns are ageless and non-attributable. A few stories are mentioned here, but the authenticity of all of them cannot be vouched for.

**PC Henry Woods
Castle Street, Worcester
February, 1926**

PC Henry Woods stood more than six-feet tall and joined the force in 1926. As he matured as a policeman so did his girth. Just about everyone knew him as 'Timber' Woods, but few would venture to estimate his weight. In 1936 he was posted to Astwood Bank and was obliged to patrol his beat on a pedal cycle. The creaks and groans from his protesting machine ensured that the locals knew where he was, well before he came into sight. The old bike regularly suffered from broken or bent spokes, a problem that persisted until Timber visited the Royal Enfield motorcycle factory in Redditch and had motorcycle spokes fitted to it.

Following the death of a police pensioner in a village near Kidderminster, some of the Kidderminster police afternoon shift were allowed to attend his funeral. When the service had finished, the mourners, including the policemen, gathered around the grave and watched the coffin being lowered. The policemen stood to attention holding their helmets under their arms. One officer relaxed his grip for a moment and several dozen pairs of eyes watched his helmet roll slowly over the edge of the grave and engage in a race with the casket to its final resting place. The helmet won. A highly embarrassed policeman asked the undertakers if they could lift the coffin out again so he could retrieve his helmet. When this was done, a search party was sent to look for a ladder so that the muddy helmet could be recovered. It was some time before the solemn proceedings could continue.

Policemen who breached the rules were often banished to Oldbury, which became known for a number of years as a punishment station. An added punishment was the canteen food. The lady-cook in the 1920s reputedly enjoyed liquid refreshment so much that she generally failed to fulfil her housekeeping duties. However, when dignitaries visited the station she was keen to create a favourable view of her work, and allowed the smell of cooking onions to permeate the premises. Important visitors never failed to be suitably impressed by the perceived, pleasant dining arrangements.

Drill has been a feature of police training since the 1830s. It was designed to instil a sense of smartness and uniformity into new recruits. It also allowed bodies of police officers to move quickly and efficiently on those occasions when larger than usual numbers were needed at times of disturbance or during a parade. Nowadays, it is rarely seen in public, but, prior to the 1960s and 1970s it was not at all uncommon.

On one occasion in 1927, a new recruit, PC William Gummery was fitted out with a second-hand uniform that had seen better days and was polluted with the smell of mothballs. A few days later he was receiving drill instruction, on the backyard of the police headquarters. As he and his colleagues were ordered to 'about turn', they all stamped their feet in unison and the buttons securing Bill's braces to his trousers flew off. His trousers immediately fell about his ankles, much to the amusement of his colleagues and a group of female observers.

In another incident, at Evesham the superintendent, Edward McDonaugh, was determined to impose his will upon the men in his division. It has been said that his predecessor, Superintendent Alfred Pass, a far gentler personality, had allowed the division to become rather lax. McDonaugh decided that each of his sergeants should be capable of taking over the drill instruction as part of his drive for discipline. To help him with his plans, he enlisted the help of Sergeant William Robinson from Broadway. Robinson was at least as ferocius as McDonaugh, and barked his commands on the yard at the back of the Abbey Road police station in Evesham, as the men shuffled and marched back and forth.

To ensure the uniform movement of a body of marching men, it is customary to convey the words of command loudly, but using familiar language. On many occasions Sergeant Robinson dispensed with the cautionary words normally given before the commands, such as 'parade' or 'squad', and this often led to the men's movements being made on the wrong foot with catastrophic results as far as uniformity and smartness were concerned.

One afternoon, McDonaugh instructed Sergeant John Heath from Pershore, to take over the instructions from Sergeant Robinson, who had set the men marching towards a fence on the other side of the yard. Sergeant Heath, for some reason, could not remember any words of command. He watched as the group of policemen headed for the fence, unable to stop or turn them. The front row of policemen knew enough to stop at the fence, 'marking time'– (marching on the spot). The only instruction Sergeant Heath was able to utter was a plaintive "Come back." Most people on the yard thought that this was extremely funny and reacted predictably. However, Superintendent McDonaugh exploded in a rage which created even greater hilarity.

Around the turn of the century there was an old warehouse, near to the police station at Dudley, that went up in flames. The police fire brigade was soon on the scene, under the command of the chief superintendent. It took about an hour or so to extinguish the fire, and when the job was done the firemen retired to a favourite pub in New Street. Sitting in the corner, having a nap, was the policeman who was supposed to be patrolling the beat where the fire had occurred. His colleagues quickly told him what had happened and he hurried away. A short time later the chief superintendent came across the officer, standing in Wolverhampton Street, animatedly directing traffic away from the scene of the fire. Clearly impressed, the senior officer released him to his normal duties and, to the officer's embarrassment, congratulated him in front of his colleagues a few days later at a pay parade.

In 1939, PC James Lancaster was stationed at Redditch. He lived in the single quarters, which were close to the superintendent's house and garden. The single men were ordered to be in their quarters by 11.30p.m. each night. This instruction tended to interfere with Jim's social engagements, and on more than one occasion he had been caught returning late. All sorts of methods were tried by the single men to beat the system. Windows were left insecure with dangling ropes or knotted sheets and doors were left unlocked, but Sergeant James Brunt was wise to them all and routinely carried out late-night checks. One night, PC George Chesworth, who also lived in the quarters, waited until the sergeant had done his rounds, and then went and opened a window for his colleague. In preparation, Jim Lancaster had left the superintendent's ladder on the ground outside the window. When he returned from his evening out, he propped the ladder against the wall and climbed in. To hide the fact that he had got in this way, he pushed the ladder away from the window, with the intention that it fell close to the wall. Sod's Law took over and the ladder fell and flattened the superintendent's dahlias. On a scale of criminality, this was indeed close to murder. Only a short time elapsed before PC Lancaster became Mr Lancaster.

When PC Richard Shaw joined the force in 1966 he was keen to impress and hung onto every word that his senior colleagues uttered. An older constable was appointed to show Dick the ropes, but the opportunity to tease a new recruit was too good to miss. One day as they both patrolled Church Street, Malvern, the experienced officer spotted a motor car at the traffic lights. Quickly he drew the younger officer back to the Woolworths doorway and pointed to the car. "You are very lucky," he said. "Your first few days on the streets and here comes the chief constable. Take your timing from me, march to the edge of the pavement and throw him one up. It'll be a feather in your cap." The younger officer watched the lights change and the motor car came towards them. From the corner of his eye he saw his colleague start to move forward. He strode smartly to the edge of the pavement, came to attention, up two three, down two three, he saluted. At that moment the motor car, an old and battered Morris Minor, crawled past, being driven by a lady aged about eighty, with her hat rammed firmly on her head, gripping the steering wheel with a great determination. As she crashed through the gears she stared at the young policeman, showing complete indifference to his gesture of respect. Back at the Woolworths doorway, the other policeman was uncontrollable.

In 1912 Superintendent William (Hooky) Walker was paying his usual monthly visit to Abberley police cottage to see PC Richard Jackson. He arrived in a one-horse gig driven by a uniformed policeman. As he knocked at the front door of the station he was quite unaware that he had a nickname. Young Emma Jackson answered and shouted over her shoulder to her mother, "Mum, it's Mr Hooky". Some embarrassing explanations ensued, followed by a severe ticking off for Emma.

**Superintendent William (Hooky) Walker at the
Shirehall, Worcester on 14th October, 1912
displaying his Police Coronation Medal.**

Early in the 1960s, Sergeant John Lampitt, commonly known as Jack, was the force-training sergeant, based at headquarters. Jack was provided with a gleaming Royal Enfield 'Bullet' motorcycle to get around the county, and it was his pride and joy. Police cadets stationed at headquarters were trained to ride motorcycles in order to deliver despatches. They were provided with BSA Bantam machines, but the Bantams did not cut a dash, like the Bullet. The cadets took every opportunity to ride the sergeant's motorcycle, generally without his knowledge. The youngsters imagined themselves at the T.T. races, leaning the machine, first to the left then to right. It was no surprise, therefore, that the Bullet often returned to the garage with a scraped fairing. Each time this happened, emergency repairs were called for, before the fierce sergeant looked for the culprits.

Police cadets

The Police Cadet Scheme originated during the Second World War, when young men were recruited to act as Police Auxiliary Messengers. As the name suggests, they were used to carry messages and for any other work normally given to an office junior. When the Messengers were disbanded, a similar group of youngsters was retained, dressed in civilian clothes, and called boy clerks. As time went on, the force began to realise that the young men, and later young women, provided a useful source of recruitment to the regulars. With government support, the cadet scheme was set on a formal footing and its members were issued with a distinctive uniform. Although they had no police powers, these young people were given the opportunity to work alongside regular police officers. Cadets joined, aged between sixteen and eighteen. They had opportunities for further education, outward-bound training, and spending time with other organisations, including the probation service and hospitals.

Police dogs

In 1952 Superintendent William Gibson of Redditch encouraged the chief constable to introduce dog handlers to the force. Gibson's research into the subject had revealed that the Surrey Constabulary, which was one of the leading authorities in this field, had a number of puppies available for purchase at fifteen guineas each. Approval was given to buy two puppies.

Detective Superintendent William Gibson
c1962

Two officers were selected to become trainee dog handlers. They were PC Norman Baylis and PC Joseph Bradley. Baylis was given a Doberman Pinscher dog puppy named 'Pedro', and Bradley received a German Shepherd bitch puppy named 'Quetta'. Both officers were posted to the Mayfields police station at Redditch, where they were required to spend four hours patrolling the beat and four hours exercising, grooming and feeding their animals. PC Stanley Sheldon, whose civilian trade was a joiner, built two kennels to house the dogs. He later constructed hurdles, ladders, plank walks and other training paraphernalia for the dogs and their handlers.

Pc Joseph Bradley with Police Dog Quetta
Mayfields, Redditch c1953

Once the men and their dogs had completed their training, their sponsors were keen to see impressive results. Unfortunately, success was slow in coming and interest was beginning to wane. On 31st August 1954, Norman Baylis was called to Hewell Grange borstal near Redditch. Two inmates named Adams and Ruane had absconded and Pedro was required to track them. The dog and his handler set off at a brisk pace across country. He tracked for some considerable distance before he found the youngsters hiding in a coppice near Bromsgrove. At last the senior officers who had supported the venture could afford a little self-congratulation.

On 2nd August 1958, Quetta produced a litter of puppies. There were five dogs and five bitches, all of which were strong and healthy. Two days later all the puppies were dead. Post mortems revealed that they had died from infective hepatitis. These deaths caused severe disappointment, not least because two of the puppies would have been used to develop the force 'dog section', as it became known. There was more sadness to come. On 11th August 1958, Pedro was confirmed to be suffering from hardpad and was deteriorating. By 6th September the situation had become hopeless and Pedro had to be put to sleep.

In spite of these setbacks, the dog section continued and within a few years there was a dog handler stationed in each division, with a Sergeant dog handler in charge of the section.

Cyprus

The island of Cyprus became the focus of attention in 1955 when the guerrilla war there forced the British government to declare a state of emergency. Archbishop Makarios was the leader of the enosis movement, which was trying to negotiate a union between the island and Greece. When his efforts failed, right-wing extremists turned to violence to achieve their ends. In 1956 British police officers were drafted in and were known as the Cyprus Police UK Unit.

Amongst the first group to go in August 1956 was a Worcestershire contingent that included PC Daniel Nash, PC Donald Young, PC Ivor Webb, PC John Coombe and PC Leonard Fraser. Each constable was given the temporary rank of sergeant, and drew a sergeant's second-hand uniform from the stores.

PC Daniel Nash poses beside his Austin Westminster patrol car at The Squires, Evesham, c1960

The conditions of service in Cyprus included a two-year contract that comprised twenty-one months on active service followed by three months leave in the United Kingdom. Officers were allowed fourteen days' leave each year locally, but there were no rest days. The purple and green General Service Medal was awarded to all police personnel who served in Cyprus during the troubles.

A number of British policemen were killed and wounded in Cyprus. Soon after his arrival PC Ivor Webb was shot and seriously wounded. By arrangement, he had gone to a local camera shop with some of his colleagues. Two terrorist gunmen lay in wait for them and there was an exchange of fire in which Webb was injured. The terrorists were later named as Nicos Sampson and Athos Petrides. Sampson worked for a local newspaper and returned to the scene a few moments later to take photographs' which were subsequently featured in newspapers all over the world.

On 29th October 1956, the chief constable reported to the police authority that PC Webb had sustained wounds in six places and was in hospital. His doctors were said to be satisfied with his progress. By 17th December he was fit and well, and back on duty.

Police officers out and about

Every police officer worth his or her salt knows of a place on their beat where it is possible to get a cup of tea and 'a warm'. Often there is more than one, and in police terminology these places are known as tea-stops. Supervisory officers know they exist, but most turn a blind eye if they are used sensibly. Indeed, it was not unknown for the deputy chief constable to meet motor patrol officers at a café on Brockeridge Common in the 50s and 60s, and treat them to a cup of tea.

Before the advent of personal radios, contact with the patrolling officer was maintained by making points, generally at public telephone boxes at set times. At Droitwich, on nights, it became routine to visit a packaging company situated on a small trading estate on the outskirts of the town. The factory was surrounded by a high wire fence, and a handful of gravel thrown onto the roof would alert the night watchman to the officer's arrival. When the gates were unlocked, the policeman could enjoy a few minutes rest and a hot drink whilst he waited for a call from the police station.

Sometimes night duty was not so comfortable for the police officer. In April 1957, PC Gordon Mandell was on night duty, examining lock-up premises at Oldbury. He went to the rear of some offices and noticed that two panes of glass had been broken in a window. When he looked closer he could see that there was a man inside. The officer told him to come out but the man refused. Mandell went to the front of the building, where he saw two members of the public, Mr and Mrs Gerald Fathom. PC Mandell asked Mr Fathom to remain where he was whilst Mrs Fathom went to get assistance. The constable then returned to the rear of the building, to be met by the burglar climbing out onto the window sill and jumping to the ground. As he did so he struck out at the policeman, hitting him over the left eye with a brandy bottle. The force of the blow was such that the bottle broke, leaving Mandell blinded and dazed.

Mr Fathom heard the noise from the scuffle and saw a man running towards him. He tackled the man and held on to him until the officer had gathered his senses and could assist. Although PC Mandell was bleeding profusely and could not see properly, he managed to handcuff the burglar. When the officer later received medical treatment, the wound to his head required four stitches.

The trial judge told PC Mandell, "You have behaved with great courage and presence of mind in this case." To Mr Fathom he said, "I would like to take this opportunity of saying how courageous and proper your conduct was in this case, and also that of your wife. You behaved in the highest way that citizens can in cases like this."

One night in October 1957 PC Frederick Smith was in the process of checking the security of the railway-station goods yard at Hinton on the Green, near Evesham. He discovered two men in the signal box. Smith arrested both men and placed them in his police car. As he was about to drive away, the prisoner in the front seat attacked him and was able to escape. Subsequently this man was recaptured in Birmingham and a third man was arrested in Wolverhampton. All three men had been stealing drums of copper wire belonging to the Midlands Electricity Board, and they were later sentenced to two years' imprisonment.

Situations can change in a matter of moments for police officers, as PC Donald Ackerman and PC Dennis Collins of Langley found out. One minute they were having a quiet cup of tea at the police station, the next they were on their way to the home of a George Spriggs, who had apparently gone berserk. He was said to be brandishing a bread knife, and his children were alone at home with him. His wife had run out of the house to seek help. By the time the officers arrived on the scene, Spriggs was standing in the middle of the road swinging a bicycle chain in one hand whilst brandishing a bread knife in the other. When attempts at negotiation have failed, modern policing techniques would have led to the man being incapacitated by a spray or cornered with riot shields. In this case the policemen only had truncheons at their disposal, and had to rely on their own ingenuity and personal strength to overpower the man. Spriggs was later examined by a doctor and removed to a mental hospital.

There are times when members of the public have to decide whether or not to take matters into their own hands. Duncan Wooldridge of Pedmore was faced with such a decision. On 28th April 1957, he was playing tennis at the North Worcestershire Tennis Club in Stourbridge when his attention was drawn to another member's motor car being driven away. He saw that it was not the owner in the car but two young men, and decided to give chase in his own vehicle. He was eventually able to turn in front of the stolen car and stop it. There was a collision and the stolen motor car collided with a telegraph pole. Both cars were extensively damaged. Mr Wooldridge managed to detain the driver; the passenger ran off but was arrested later. In a generous gesture, the chief constable agreed that the police would foot the bill for the repair of Mr Wooldridge's car.

Lloyd-Williams retires

After 30 years and 198 days as the chief constable of Worcestershire, Captain Evan Lloyd-Williams had to retire, as he had reached the upper age limit for a serving chief constable. He had seen the county constabulary through many difficult times and his personality had been effectively stamped on the force. Admiral Sir William Tennant said, "I feel that I am speaking not only on behalf of the Standing Joint Committee, but on behalf of the whole of the county in saying how very much the chief constable's conscientiousness and efficient service has been appreciated."

Worcestershire's last chief constable

The new chief constable was John Alexander Willison, and he took up his post on 8th April 1958.

John Willison was born in Dalry in Ayrshire on 3rd January 1914. He joined the City of London police in 1933 and was promoted to sergeant six years later. In 1943 he joined the Royal Naval Volunteer Reserve (R.N.V.R.) as a seaman. In April the following year he joined H.M.S. Sylvia and was later commissioned as a temporary sub-lieutenant. He was discharged from the R.N.V.R. in January 1946 and was married in 1947. When he resumed his police career he was soon promoted to inspector. He spent two years as an instructor at the Police Training School at Ryton on Dunsmore, and in July 1952 he became the chief constable of Berwick, Roxborough and Selkirk police. He held that post for six years.

Sir John Alexander Willison
Chief Constable of the Worcestershire Constabulary
1958 - 1967

Willison was an appropriate choice for chief constable. No longer was it acceptable to control his subordinates with a heavy hand, and his was certainly a gentler touch. Members of the Police Federation negotiating team found that he was a man with whom they could do business, and between them many useful changes were achieved.

New-style uniforms

By the end of the decade, for the first time constables and sergeants began to wear open-necked tunics instead of jackets with upright collars. The lower ranks wore blue shirts and black ties, while inspectors and above wore white shirts and black ties. A consequence of this change was that constables' and sergeants' 'collar numbers' were now displayed on shoulder epaulettes.

County motorways

In November 1960 the first motorway in the county, the M50, was officially opened. Worcestershire, Herefordshire and Gloucestershire police each took equal turns to patrol the M50. Their eight-hour day began from Hindlip Hall, in specially adapted police cars. The vehicles were equipped with larger than normal fuel tanks, and by, removing the rear seats, extra equipment could be crammed in. Their crews could not leave the twenty-one-mile section of road, known as 'the strip', until they were relieved by colleagues. There were no emergency telephones and, in the case of breakdown or an accident, motorists usually had to wait until a police patrol passed by.

In an article published in the *Evesham Journal* in 1981, Superintendent Daniel Nash, who as a Police Constable was an early member of the motorway patrol, recalled cooking his meals over a watchman's brazier at the side of the carriageway. He said how saddened he was to see how the wildlife suffered as foxes and badgers stubbornly refused to change their routes and were knocked down as they crossed the road.

During the first half of the 1960s, the M5 was built from Strensham to Lydiate Ash and then on to Quinton. The construction of this highway coincided with the installation of various new warning signs including 'accident' and 'skid risk'. These warning signs could be switched on as required, by staff at the headquarters information room, whilst new 'fog' signs could be operated by the police patrols at affected locations.

The patrol cars were expected to cover about 80,000 miles in their police lifetime, before being sold or traded in. The police used a variety of different makes of vehicle, and some, usually Vauxhalls, failed to achieve their target mileage economically, costing more than other police vehicles in repair costs and down time. When the Austin A95 Westminster was introduced to the force, it seemed that at last there was a suitable police car. Built especially for police work and equipped with an A105 engine with a direct gear change, it looked the part and was, arguably, one of the best police cars ever to have been produced.

Police bravery

Throughout the 1960s, county police officers continued to show their mettle, sometimes in the most trying situations. In February 1961, Sergeant Leslie Whyle, PC Robin Smith and PC Frederick Rutter were called to a foundry at Halesowen. They found that a fitter, William Homer, had been fitting a connection to a gas main and had been overcome by gas. One of his workmates, Jack Street, tried to help him, but his attempts failed. He then called for help from the police. When he got back to the foundry he also collapsed. In spite of the strong possibility of an explosion, the policemen dragged the unconscious men clear of the danger and began to administer artificial respiration. As a result, both men survived. Each officer was awarded Royal Humane Testimonials on Vellum.

In the early hours of an October day in 1965, police officers were called to the West Midlands Gas Board premises in Redditch. A man had been seen climbing a gas holder and was at a height of some sixty feet from the ground. The man ignored requests to come down and continued to climb higher. PC David Paterson began to climb up the gas holder towards him. Meanwhile a colleague went to get help from the fire brigade. By the time the fire crew arrived, PC Paterson was about eighty feet from the ground and the man was nearby, threatening to throw himself off. The police officer was able to establish a dialogue with him, and after about ninety minutes managed to persuade him to climb down. The conditions that the policeman had been working under were treacherous. It was extremely dark and cold, and the ladders and cat walks he had used were only nine inches wide. In 1966 PC Paterson received a Queen's Commendation for his bravery.

On two occasions in 1967, PC Robert Thomson, the Wolverley policeman, carried out acts that warranted awards from two different organisations. The first occurrence involved rescuing sheep from the River Stour at Wolverley, for which he received a framed Certificate of Merit from the R.S.P.C.A. for his courage and humanity. The second incident concerned his rescue of a man who fell into a canal lock at Wolverley. Sadly the man did not survive. The Royal Humane Society awarded PC Thomson with a Testimonial on Parchment.

A new police station at Malvern

On 29th June 1964, a new police station at Malvern was officially opened by the Home Secretary, the Right Honourable Henry Brooke P.C. MP. The complex included police offices, a magistrates court and an ambulance station. It was quite a lavish occasion with more than a hundred dignitaries in attendance. There was a parade of regular and special constables to the musical accompaniment of the Band of the Lancashire Fusiliers.

The new building was built on sloping ground situated between Victoria Road and Albert Road North. Access to the police station and magistrates court was from Victoria Road, whilst the lower level, which gave access to an extensive car park, housed the ambulance station. The police club also opened onto the car park.

Not everyone was impressed with the new building. Mary Woolston, a former resident of Malvern, wrote to a local newspaper, from New Zealand. She was appalled at the building's ugliness and described it as a cross between a collection of council flats and a nineteenth century workhouse. She advised that the complex should be hidden behind Chinese poplars, which she hoped would grow to eighty feet.

Reduction in the working week

On 1st July 1964, the working week for police officers was reduced from forty-four to forty-two hours. This resulted in an additional rest day each month. Senior police officers went through a routine that has nowadays become second nature; juggling staff numbers to try and get more from less. An unknown inspector committed the following observations to paper in respect of Kent Road section, which was part of the Halesowen sub-division. His sentiments have been expressed many times since, both inside and outside the service.

"The public have a right to service and protection and the only way to give this service is to have enough men to give it. There are roads in this borough, particularly at Kent Road, where they never see a policeman from one years end to another and that is one of the obvious reasons why crime is rising and still rising, because there are not enough patrol men about and seen to be about to deter offenders. I think if more attention were given to getting men on the beat on foot and less attention given to chasing round in motor cars the more efficient the service would become. I am not suggesting that we do away with area cars, but they in themselves are not enough without the substantial addition of foot patrol men to cope with modern day requirements."

A Police Authority

The Police Act of 1964 abolished the Standing Joint Committee and replaced it with a Police Authority that was made up of two-thirds county council members and one-third magistrates. The total number of members was set by the county council. The creation of a police authority with a majority of politicians was seen by many as a step towards making the new committee and, as a consequence, the police force more accountable to the public. The Authority took up its duties on 1st June 1965.

A new police force

On 1st April 1966, the borough of Oldbury, comprising the Oldbury and Warley police sub-divisions, was incorporated into the new borough of Warley. Warley joined with four other boroughs, including Dudley, and a new police force called the West Midlands Police was formed. Sixty-nine officers from Worcestershire transferred to the West Midlands Police and a further seven joined later. Fifty-seven special constables also transferred.

The remainder of the force also faced minor adjustments. The police station at Cofton Hackett was transferred to the Birmingham police. Amblecote, formerly in Staffordshire, along with Halesowen, became part of the Stourbridge division.

The Hindlip fire

During the morning of 18th October 1966, a fire broke out at Hindlip Hall. Painters were working on the top floor of the building, burning off old paint. Although the painter concerned was unaware, the heat generated by the blow lamp he was using ignited wooden lathes in the cavity wall. Fanned by a strong wind, the flames destroyed the roof, the top floor and the floor timbers of part of the top floor.

Hindlip Hall c1947
Former Headquarters of the Worcestershire Constabulary
and now the West Mercia Constabulary HQ

All personnel were evacuated, and then formed into work parties to help rescue furniture, equipment and records. Everyone, from police cadets to the chief constable, lent a hand. Apart from the structural damage, the personal property of the cadets and the contents of the sports stores were completely destroyed. Firemen and appliances were called in from Worcester, Droitwich and Bromsgrove to deal with the blaze, which took more than two hours to bring under control.

The consequences of the fire were also serious. Water seeped into communications equipment and the information room was unable to function. An emergency communications system set up in a police caravan parked nearby provided radio contact with police vehicles, but the emergency telephone system on the motorways was out of commission. Extra police vehicles patrolled the motorways to assist members of the public in difficulties, and when the Automobile Association became aware of the problems, it provided extra motorway patrols as well.

Water damage was not limited to the information room equipment. Elsewhere in the building, water soaked through into lower rooms, and the police borrowed a variety of heaters to help dry out these areas. In one case, a RAF hot-air drier burst into flames and the fire brigade had to rush back to put that fire out.

Repairs to the Hall were estimated to be in the region of £50,000, but it was agreed that it would be beneficial to add another 4,500 square feet of floor space by building an extra storey. For the outlay of an additional £23,000 it was possible to restore the building, add an extra floor, provide a new staircase and lift, and install oil-fired central heating, a new telephone exchange and a vehicle disposition board for the information room.

The end of the Worcestershire Constabulary

On 18th May 1966, the Home Secretary announced that the number of police forces in England and Wales would be reduced from 117 to 49, and this would be achieved by a series of amalgamations. The police authorities of Worcestershire, Herefordshire, Shropshire and Worcester City chose to amalgamate voluntarily. John Willison was appointed the chief constable of the new force, which was christened 'West Mercia Constabulary'. Hindlip Hall was chosen as the headquarters, and an insignia was designed to incorporate features contained in each of the amalgamating forces' County or City Arms.

The date for the amalgamation was set for 1st October 1967, and representatives of each of the constituent forces met frequently in the run up to that date, to decide on everything from the uniform to be worn, to the choice of forms to be used. Nothing escaped attention.

When the West Mercia Constabulary opened its doors for business, it was short of 137 officers, but, for those policemen and women who were qualified for promotion and prepared to move, there were unprecedented opportunities. Whilst many individuals benefited from their promotion, the force also achieved integration without the need for compulsory moves across the board. Meanwhile, the Worcestershire Constabulary was no more. As an Organisation it had been in existence for almost 128 years. Its officers had served the county with dedication, in many instances showing outstanding commitment and courage.

John Willison continued to lead the new force until he retired in 1974. During his tenure, and since, the police force has been subjected to many upheavals. New initiatives have come and gone, although some old-stagers would say there are no new ideas, just old ones re-invented. However, as successive governments introduce fresh legislation, with associated procedures and constraints, and police personnel contort themselves to pursue current thinking, few stop to assess the consequences of what has gone before.

Index

A

Ackerman, PC Donald 147
Agg, PC James, 52
Allen, PC Frederick, 93
Allez, Supt Peter, 12
Andrews, Sgt George, 98
Arton, Insp William, 18
Ashmore, Sp Con Albert,*125*
Askew, PC Albert, 71
Aston, PC Richard, 58
Attwood, PC George, 22

B

Ballard, PC Ralph, *105*
Banks, PC William, 67
Bateman, PC John, 51
Baylis, PC Norman,*126*,*127*, 144, 145
Bayliss, PC Charles, 56
Bedford, PC Henry, 52
Beesley, PC Garfield, 31
Benbow, PC George, 139
Berry, PC William, 81
Best, PC William, 72
Bevan, Supt John, 21, 24, 28
Biddle, PC George, 68
Blower, Sgt Alfred, *129*
Bradley, PC Jonathon, 19
Bradley, PC Joseph, 144
Bradshaw, PC Thomas, 19
Brecknell, PC Richard, 22
Brereton, PC Henry, 35
Broadhurst, PC William, 28
Brown, PC James, 37
Brunt, Sgt James, 142
Bryan, Sgt John, 131
Bullock, PC Roger, 78
Burton, Supt Henry, 14, 21, 31, 96
Butler, PC Charles, 72

C

Calder, WPC Phyllis, *109*
Carmichael, Lt Col G L, 35, 47, 49, 51, 70, 73, 86,
Chesworth, PC George, 142
Clark, PC Alfred, 68
Clarke, PC Charles, 90
Clarke, PC Peter, 58
Clarke, PC Thomas, 53
Clinton, PC George, 64
Colley, Sgt John, 40
Collins, PC Dennis, 147
Cook, Det Con Colin, *125*
Coombe, PC John, 145
Cooper, PC William, 77
Cooper, Sgt William, 65, 98
Cope, Supt William, 73
Craig, Supt William, 17

D

Dainty, Insp Richard, *120*
Davies, Det Sgt George, 27
Davis, PC Edward, 12
Davis, PC Franklin, 138
Davis, PC James, 41, 43, 56
Davis, PC Samuel, 53
Doorbar, PC J, 37
Drew, PC Arthur, 76
Drury, Sgt Charles, 38, 40, 52
Dumbleton, PC James, 65,76

E

Edwards, PC George, 31
Ellison, PC George, 53

F

Farmer, Supt William, 86
Fitzer, PC William, 65
Ford, Pol War Res George, *129*
Forty, Supt William, 22
Fraser, PC Leonard, 145

G

Gall, PC Thomas, 53
Gibson, Supt William, 109, 144
Gittus, PC Ernest, 63
Gray, PC Robert, *119*
Gray, Sgt Sidney, *119*
Gray, Supt Gustavus, *119*
Green, PC John, 77
Greet, PC Bennet, *123*
Griffin, PC John, 77
Griffiths, PC Edward, 52
Gummery, PC Harry, 89
Gummery, PC William, 141

H

Hadley, PC Edward, 63
Hall, PC Ishmael, 67
Hanley, Sgt William, 62
Harris, PC Thomas, 58
Harris, R R, 9, 25, 33, 36, 45
Harris, Sgt Thomas, 98
Harris, Supt William, 23
Hartland, PC Herbert, 67
Harvey, PC John, 52
Hayes, PC Frederick, 90, 92
Haynes, PC Harvey, 92
Haynes, PC Moses, 43
Heath Sgt John, 139,141
Hemming, PC John, 65
Hemming, PC Reginald, *115*
Hill, PC John, 66
Hill, PC Stanley, *117*
Hinde, Supt Thomas, 89
Homer, PC Walter, *129*
Hooper, PC Henry, 51
Hudspith, PC Edward, 37
Hughes, PC John, 13

I

Inight, Det Supt S, 122, *126*, 133

J

Jackson, PC Richard, 142
James, PC Frederick, 93
Jeffrey, Supt William, 31, 41
Jeffs, PC Richard, *108*
Jennings, PC John, 72
Jewkes, Supt Joseph, 96
Jones, PC Alfred, 67
Jones, PC George, 51
Jones, PC Walter, 78
Jones, WPC Margaret, *109*

K

Kemp, Supt Henry, 45, 47, 49
Kennard, PC Walter, 72
Kennedy, PC Angus, 19
King, PC Harry, 81
King, Supt James, 15

L

Lampitt, Sgt John, 143
Lancaster, PC James, 142
Lane, PC John, 29
Lane, Supt John, 14
Leech, PC John, 24
Littlefield, PC Charles, 51
Lloyd - Williams, Capt J E, 75, 109, *118*, *121*, *125*, 137, 148
Lloyd, R J (DCC), 33
Lovejoy, PC John, 78
Lowe, PC Reginald, 139
Ludlow, PC Thomas, 19
Lyes, Supt William, *106*

M

Mandell, PC Gordon, 146
Mann, PC William, 72
Mantle, PC George, 37
Manton, Supt William, 12
Martin, PC Thomas, 28
Mason, PC Joseph, 51
Masters, Sgt Charles, *127*
McDonaugh PC Edward, 77, 141
Middleton, PC William, *123*
Milsom, Supt William, *106*
Mobbs, Supt Peter, *116*, *120*
Morris, PC Oliver, 36
Moss, PC Alexander, 77

N

Narramore, Sgt Robert,53,55
Nash, PC Daniel,138,145,149
Nash, PC Solomon, 72
Nevinson, Guy Pol War Res, *125*

O

Oliver, Supt John, 32
Osborne, PC Francis, 58
Overend, Supt Miles, 35
Overton, PC Sidney, *112*
Owen, PC Frederick, *129*
Owen, PC Harry, 65

P

Pantin PC Henry, 20
Pass, PC Alfred, 70, 141
Paterson, PC David, 150
Patten, PC Henry, 68
Pennington, ThomasDCC,*115*
Peters, PC Frank, *129*
Phillips, Insp John, 18
Phillips, PC James, 72
Pitt, Insp Harold, 139
Pitt, Supt Francis, 73, 76
Poulson, PC Edward, 66
Powell, Sgt Edwin, 91
Poyner, Sgt William, 87
Pratley, PC Harry, 89
Price, Supt James, 131
Probert, PC Thomas, 77
Pugh, Supt Alfred, 55, 73
Purcer, PC Isaac, 36

Q

Quarrell, Sgt Arthur, 130

R

Raby, PC John, 12
Radford Sgt Joseph, 14
Randall, PC Philip, 29
Reeve, PC William, 28
Robinson Sgt William, 141
Rose, PC John, 28
Round, PC Benjamin, *113*
Round, PC Edward, 78
Rowley, Sgt Thomas, 29
Rudd, PC William, 36
Rudnick, Supt Charles, 101. 103
Rutter, PC Frederick, 149

S

Sandells, PC Alfred, 49
Sanders, PC Basil, 139
Sanders, PC Cyril, 108, 139
Saull, Det Sgt Charles, *125*
Shaw, PC Richard, 142
Sheldon, PC Stanley, 144
Sheppard, PC William, 41
Sherriff, PC William, 52
Short, PC Frank, 67
Sier, PC William, 19
Skerratt, PC George, *112*
Skerratt, Sgt Richard, 132
Smith, PC Eli, *123*
Smith, PC Frederick, 147
Smith, PC Robin, 149
Smith, Sgt Frederick, 87,106
Speke, Ch Supt R, 98,
Spiers, PC Benjamin, 19
Squires, PC William, 58
Stafford, PC Eli, 93
Staite, PC Thomas, 31
Stanford, PC Charles, 36
Stanton, PC William, 19

T

Taylor, PC John, 58
Thomson, PC Robert, 150
Timms, PC Thomas, 84
Turner, Sgt John, 22
Tyler, Alfred DCC, 41, 56

W

Wainwright, Insp George, 98
Waldron, PC Michael, 52
Walker, Lt Col H S, 73, 84, 108, 117
Walker, Supt William, 142
Wall, PC Arthur, 72
Wallace Det Insp Thomas,50
Walters, PC Jared, 67
Wargent, PC Albert, 48
Warmington, PC Stephen, 35
Warner, PC Leslie, *115*
Wasley, James DCC, 59, 73, 78, 80, 86
Webb PC George, 130
Webb, PC Cyril, *127*
Webb, PC Ivor, 145
Wheeler, John DCC, 69
Wheeler, PC John, *115*
White, PC/Fireman William, 95
Whitehouse, PC Frederick,41
Whitmore, PC John, 35
Whyle, Sgt Leslie, 149
Williams, Det Insp Thomas, 122, 134
Williams, PC Edward, *115*
Williams, PC Thomas, 58
Willison, J A, 148, 153
Woods, PC Henry, 140
Woodward, PC Robert, 20

Y

Young PC Charles, 49
Young, PC Donald, 145